Library of
Davidson College

DIVINATION IN THAILAND

By the same author
SIAMESE STATE CEREMONIES
THE UNIVERSE AROUND THEM
etc.

DIVINATION IN THAILAND

*The hopes and fears of a
Southeast Asian people*

H. G. QUARITCH WALES

CURZON PRESS

First published 1983
Curzon Press Ltd: London and Dublin
© H. G. Quaritch Wales 1981
0 7007 0147 8

291.3
W172d

83-9594
Printed in Hungary

CONTENTS

	INTRODUCTION	vii
I	FIRST CLUES	1
II	LIFE'S PROMISE	8
III	THE MORE IMMEDIATE	36
IV	PALMISTRY	52
V	MARRIAGE PARTNERS	63
VI	A HOME OF ONE'S OWN	72
VII	AGRICULTURE AND TRADE	87
VIII	LOST, STOLEN OR STRAYED	104
IX	DREAMS	116
X	DAYS OF DESTINY	123
XI	WARS AND RUMOURS OF WARS	132
	GLOSSARY	143
	INDEX	144

LIST OF ILLUSTRATIONS

Between pages 66 and 67

I   Year of the Horse (see p. 14), from British Library MS. Or. 13650. The year *devatā* is not in this MS. shown riding the Horse, but is seated near the year tree (banana). These are balanced by four horse figures, each with a caption giving the nature of the horse during the quarter. The circular plan at top right indicates numerically the relation of the planetary deities to the human microcosm.

II   Year of the Monkey (see p. 15), from the same MS. Here the demon year-spirit stands near the year-tree (Jack).

III-VIII   Predictions of six of the Twelve Years, from British Library MS. Or. 3593 (Satow MS.). For each year the illustrations run downwards, from top left: months 5 or 11, 6 or 12, 7 or 1; and from top right: 8 or 2, 9 or 3, 10 or 4. Occasionally the illustrations differ from those described in our text, but have the same significance.

III   Year of the Rat (see p. 19)

IV   Year of the Ox (see p. 20)

V   Year of the Tiger (see p. 20)

VI   Year of the Small Snake (see p. 21)

VII   Year of the Monkey (see p. 22)

VIII   Year of the Dog (see p. 23)

IX   The so-called 'Signs of the Zodiac' from British Library MS. Or. 13650. From *stūpa* (bottom row, second from left) a man counts anti-clockwise through silver umbrella, gold umbrella, decapitated person, palace, golden shrine, Rāhu, Devacara (here *devatā* on tortoise), prisoner wearing cangue, sorcerer, sorceress, *nāgarāja*, (see pp. 32–4).

X   The entwined *nāgas*, from British Library MS. Or. 13650 (see p. 66)

XI   A happy human marriage—a serene old age; but if one marries a demoness ... see Chapter V.

INTRODUCTION

Half a century ago I wrote of the Siamese royal ceremonies as I had known and studied them, their lustre as yet undimmed. It was indeed generally accepted that the very safety of the state depended on their punctual performance. But I was writing on the eve of a change of regime. Since the fateful year 1932 Siam, now Thailand, has certainly moved a very long way from absolute monarchy. But whatever is to be her ultimate political fate, whatever is to be the future status of the Buddhist religion, belief in the power of the supernatural to order the affairs of daily life is too deeply ingrained to be easily uprooted. To know what the future holds—both personally and for their country—will remain a consuming need for most Thais. In the West the present boom in astrology has answered a similar need. But astrology makes little appeal to the Thai temperament.

I am here referring to astrology in the strict sense, the deductions to be made from the position of the planets in relation to one another, to the zodiacal signs and to the observer. Such deductions had not for many centuries been founded on direct observations but on tabulated records, nowadays replaced by the astronomical calendars (ephemerides) everywhere available. From the early days of Thai independence in the fourteenth century A.D. Indian astrologers had been employed at the royal courts to work the water-clocks and fix auspicious days. They were quite capable of calculating solar and lunar eclipses. Down to modern times an astrologer (no longer a Brahman) provided the king each year with a volume of prognostications based on the royal horoscope, while at the present time an astrological almanac rivalling *Old Moore* is published for a wider public.

From the advertisements in Bangkok one might get the impression that astrology, now brought into line with modern standards and so of no special interest, is as popular as in the West; most people of any standing can show you their horoscope, and are careful to have the exact times of their children's births recorded.[1] But this is a partial view. In fact astrology remains an exotic luxury, accessible to relatively few of the country's forty-two millions and then secondary to the well-tried traditional methods of divination. It is these alone that reveal the depths of the Thai ethos, and from an angle that has so far been completely neglected. Such traditional divination remains persistently on the astrological fringe.

By this I mean basically that the Thai very generally feel that our lives are ordered rather by the planetary deities than by the planets as cosmic principles. These deities act sometimes in association with other Hindu or local animistic *devatā*, a more religious attitude than is catered for by scientific astrology. The planetary deities are usually seven in number, but nine if the shadowy planets Rāhu and Ketu are included. They make known their intentions and give us warnings either by spontaneous omens or by omens that are solicited by the diviners. The symbolic association of ideas that govern the omens are a parallel to those which we often find in magic, though magic as such is not here concerned.[2] Some of the methods used are complex, being derived from more than one source, and then modified locally; while a desire for more detailed interpretations inevitably leads to numerical elaboration, which however I shall not follow to the extreme. On the other hand some methods of divination used are very simple, and what the anthropological textbooks would describe as 'universal *in one form or another*'. It is the latter part of this phrase that cannot be ignored. For while I would not ascribe much of interest to the rattling of numbered sticks to be seen at any temple fair, it is still only lot casting (sortilege) in one form or another that gives such ingenious variations on an old theme and such fascinating artistic expressions as are to be seen in the so-called 'zodiac' and the entwined serpents illustrated in Plates IX and X.

I have discussed the question of present-day credibility of traditional divination recently with several educated, though not too westernized, Thai in Bangkok. They told me that they personally at least 'half believe' in the popular methods, and especially those for fixing lucky days for important occasions. Such believing, or half-believing, in Bangkok is certainly not confined, as one might suppose, to the older generation. A youngish official of some standing, who had spent some time in Europe, said that while he had found the prognostications based on his astrological horoscope reasonably accurate, he still rather preferred the popular methods of divination, and assured me that that was general. Two very cogent reasons were adduced: (1) The traditional methods are simpler and can often be interpreted by the inquirer without the aid of a professional diviner. (2) Astrology, while at first sight commending itself by reason of its apparent scientific accuracy, tends to upset the inquirer by reason of its immutable fatalism. The Thai people, essentially religious in outlook, do not mind an unfavourable omen if they know they can make offerings to avert it; or they can apply for a 'second opinion' by employing one or more alternative methods. Much can be ascertained independently, but for fixing an auspicious day for a wedding or similar occasion one should always enlist the aid of a skilled soothsayer. He would probably be a senior monk or the local abbot for as we know, while the Buddha disapproved of divination, one of his chief disciples, Moggellana, was an adept, and many monks seek to follow his example.

This popular competition with sophisticated astrology is undoubtedly no new thing. In the present work I use comparative material only when it serves to throw light on Thai beliefs and practices. And just here a glance at the situation in neighbouring Burma is apposite. At the old Burmese royal court Hindu Brahman astrologers, known as *pōnnas*, were more readily recruited than was the case in Siam, for the state of Manipur adjoined Burma and indeed came under Burmese rule. 'But they are dying out and at no time did they have much influence on the astrology of the country-side... Shan soothsayers (cousins of the Thai) are considered the most learned, and all their prognostications are worked out from the *Hpēwān*.'[3] This is the well-known 12-year animal cycle which was derived from China and in which each year of the cycle is ruled over by one of twelve animals whose names are not local but appear to be derived from an early south Chinese dialect. It was introduced to the first Thai kingdom of Sukhodaya in the thirteenth century A.D. at a time when there was much intercourse with China. Employing a lunar calendar it has remained continually in popular use both in Siam and in neighbouring countries. Indeed the solar calendar, introduced by the court Brahmans for astrological purposes, has never meant much to the general public. And the Chinese influence at a more popular level is by no means confined to the calendar. We tend to think of Siam, in view of its court culture and its official Buddhist religion, as a very Indianized country; but at the popular level, and especially in the field of divination, Chinese influence, often of long standing, is much in evidence. It seems to give real meaning to the term Indo-China, in which however the imports have so long been naturalized as to acquire a distinctly local character.

For solid confirmation of the opinions above-quoted we do not have to go outside Bangkok; we get it from the printing press. It must have been in 1931 that I bought there a copy of the latest edition of *Brāhmajāti* (Destiny) which had been published in three parts over the years B.E. 2470–2475 (A.D. 1926–31), by the firm of Panit Supāpon.[4] Their combined cost was four *bāt* (then seven shillings) for 310 pages, illustrated with modern sketches, and it was the second part that provided the vital statistics that the printing was the fourteenth, and of 6,000 copies. I saw that my acquisition was a printed edition of not one but many old treatises dealing with various aspects of divination. At the time it would not have occurred to me to question whether such matters were still alive in the public interest. I knew that even in such a royal ceremony as the First Ploughing much depended in the eyes of the populace on the Minister of Agriculture's choice of skirt, and on the oxen's choice of food. I put the book aside, thinking that the contents were interesting and might repay study some day—when I had the leisure.

It was several decades before that leisure came. Early in 1980 I was in Bangkok, not visiting archaeological sites as had so usually been the purpose of my travels in Thailand over the intervening years, but to spend a couple of months examining the actual divination manuscripts or similar ones preserved in the Bangkok National Library. But before I come to that it was what met me in the bookshops, indeed wayside book-stalls, that has a bearing on our immediate point, the extent of continuing popular appeal. It appeared that my former acquisition had now been superseded by a massive quarto edition of some 800 pages which had been reprinted annually during the last six years and was offered at the very reasonable present-day price of ninety *bāt* (£2). With the same title as previously it was published 'for self-instruction' by the Śrī Mahā Bodhi Divination Institute.[5] Though swollen with a good deal of material that to me seemed extraneous it had the merit of including several texts, for instance on dreams, which might well have found a place in the earlier publication.

In the manuscript department of the Bangkok National Library the catalogue of works on divination in its widest sense, including astrology, was placed before me. The collection consisted of wellnigh a thousand volumes varying from astronomical calculations to those covering our subject matter, many of them duplicates. I contented myself, during my two months' stay, with calling for a representative cross-section, not for detailed study, which would have been unnecessary for my purpose, but merely to satisfy myself with the general authenticity of the printed versions. These would naturally differ in detail if taken from manuscripts other than those in the Library.

I should say that few of the manuscripts in the National Library antedate the nineteenth century, so much having been lost with the destruction by the Burmese of the old capital Ayudhyā in 1767. Many of those that I saw had been sadly damaged by damp and insects before being permanently safeguarded in the modern air-conditioned stores of the Library. Fortunately many of the manuscripts that interest us most, those with hand-painted miniatures of the birth and marriage treatises, continued to be made, with no decline in quality, almost to the close of the last century. Printing, which had become general about 1860, offered no acceptable alternative to the miniature painting still so widely appreciated. Thus it is that some of the best-preserved Thai manuscripts are to be found not in Bangkok but in the British Library, whither they had been brought soon after manufacture. One such manuscript *Brāhmajāti*, dated the equivalent of A.D. 1885, was brought from Bangkok and presented to the British Museum just three years later, by our then minister, Sir Ernest Satow. It is mainly from this manuscript which has illustrations in the very best style of those portions of our subject that are amenable to illustration (apart from diagrams), that I have chosen for reproduction here.

Even today it cannot be said that the products of the printing press reach every remote village. There is still scope for the manuscript, if no longer as a work of art certainly as a means of practical communication. This is confirmed by the late Phya Anuman, who has given us some admirable studies of Thai traditional life. While referring more particularly to the auspicious days for beginning farming operations, he mentions that the authoritative source material is usually available in the monasteries. 'Anyone who can read and write goes and copies it out in a Thai folding book, and it is then copied again and again. It is a book in the same category as textbooks of medicine and textbooks on methods of worshipping spirits. Textbooks of this sort are found everywhere and are called household textbooks.'[6] The contents, he adds, are often memorized. So, except for the most important occasions, it would seem that nowadays there is little need to consult a specialist soothsayer.

I wish to express my gratitude to Mr. Choosak Dipayagasorn, head of the manuscripts department of the Bangkok National Library, and to his colleague Mr. Virat Unnathornvarangkoon. Both of them gave me valuable help in resolving a number of textual problems. The plates are reproduced by courtesy of the Trustees of the British Library.

NOTES TO THE INTRODUCTION

1. In recognizing, for example, the importance of the planets Uranus, Neptune and Pluto, the modern Bangkok astrologers are adhering to the present-day Western system, not the traditional Indian. So we have here a facet of Westernization paralleling the teaching of the orthodox sciences in Thai universities.
2. B.J. Terwiel, in his very interesting book *Monks and Magic* (2nd. edn. London, 1979) has much to say on the magical aspects of Buddhism in a Thai rural community, but almost nothing on divination. However, he mentions (pp. 153 f.) the existence of certain 'handbooks' in the possession of monks and laymen.
3. Hastings' *Encyclopaedia of Religion and Ethics*, III, art. Burma, p. 29.
4. Henceforth abbreviated as *B* I, II or III.
5. Abbreviated as *BSMB*.
6. Phya Anuman Rajadhon, *Life and Ritual in Old Siam*, translated and edited by W.J. Gedney, New Haven, 1961, p. 11.

CHAPTER I

FIRST CLUES

'A little bird told me' is a saying that in the West is generally accepted to be a survival of a once widespread belief in birds acting as the messengers of the gods. So it is not at all surprising that the Thai attribute their having divined how they should comport themselves as civilized beings to the intervention of a little bird—not such a little one in this case. The myth has a Brahmanical flavour and tells only of what they were learning from Hindu sources as they penetrated into the north of Siam about the twelfth century A.D. There is nothing Buddhist about it, for it deals only with everyday life, nor does it take account of what the Thai animists may already have learnt or were going to learn from Chinese contacts. Here is the myth as told in Thai manuscripts that preserve the lore of early periods.[1]

It seems that in the comparatively primeval times when the Thai were journeying south, the world was thought to be governed by two deities. One was a supreme sky deity, Devabrahmā, the other his earthly counterpart, Lokabrahmā. I am inclined to think the latter was in fact a priest, for according to the Hindu lawgiver Manu the Brahman was a great deity. Now this one appears to have been exceptionally human, for one day when Devabrahmā came down to inquire what progress Lokabrahmā had made in inculcating the eight precepts with which he had been charged, he admitted that he had forgotten what they were. 'Then I give you a week in which to remember them, after which if you do not know them when I return I will cut off your head.' Lokabrahmā was naturally appalled. He travelled about in heaven and elsewhere for six days, asking the *devas*, but in vain for no one could enlighten him.

Back on earth Lokabrahmā lay down to rest under a big tree in which there happened to be an eagle's nest, with one young one. It was badly wanting food, but the mother bird said that she had not been able to get any meat, but tomorrow she would succeed. 'What meat will it be?' asked the chick. The mother replied that tomorrow Lokabrahmā's head would be available. 'Why?' pursued the chick. 'Because he could not remember the eight precepts' replied the mother. The chick inquired what they were, but the mother said that that was none of their business. The chick then threatened that he would die if he were not told. At this the mother became sorely afraid, and eventually she told all that she had heard from the Supreme Being.

The precepts were as follows: (1) Man must refrain from sensual pleasures on the 7th, 8th, 14th and 15th of both waxing and waning moons, also at New Year, during a moon eclipse and on a birthday. Then a good *devatā* will reside in that person and protect him, otherwise a punishing demon will gain entry. (2) When a man or woman is eating, he or she must face the east.[2] (3) When answering a call of nature that person must face west.[3] (4) When a man sleeps with a woman the latter must be on the left,[4] and she must not cross her feet. (5) The couple must each wear a separate garment at night, not one spread over both. (6) Early in the morning the protecting *devatā* is in the forehead and mouth, so one should then wash the face.[5] (7) At noon he is in the breast and heart, so one should then sprinkle water over the breast. (8) In the evening he is in the feet, so before going to bed one should wash the feet. Obedience to these precepts enables the protecting *devatā* to remain within the individual, who is then happy and safe from enemies; while any lapse allows the destructive demon to enter instead.

Naturally all this information was not lost on Lokabrahmā, resting beneath the tree. So he was able to acquit himself satisfactorily in the eyes of the Supreme Being when the latter descended next day.

Now it will have been noticed that according to the fourth precept a sleeping wife must not cross her feet. The reason for this is explained in an old treatise which gives the omens to be drawn from the manner in which a couple have been sleeping.[6] Since most positions are unlucky in one way or another it is a relief to find that they only apply to certain days of the month. Only one position is really auspicious, that in which both have the head up, but it applies to the 6th, 10th and 13th of the waxing, and 4th, 7th, 10th and 14th of the waning. If the head is bent down and legs up, on five specified dates, the wife will die first, but if the legs are down the husband will die first. This however applies only to the second of the waxing, for remember it was a Brahman who promulgated the law. Heads knocking together (applicable to no less than eleven days in a month) mean divorce likely. And to answer the question with which we began, feet crossed portends a difficult birth. But this omen applies only to the 5th waxing and 3rd waning.

A premonitory dream, often of a vividly portentous character, frequently accompanies conception, but the subject may be left until later when we consider dreams in general. However, any newly-married couple are naturally eager to know whether they are likely to have children or not, and that is one good reason for every literate home to possess a copy of the trusted handbook, for the matter is not complicated enough to require interpretation by a skilled soothsayer. It is a simple numerical operation and will introduce us to the method by which the planetary deities, seven to nine in number, can often be induced to inform us of our fate. This they do by means of the remainder that is left after they have divided a certain number representing the particular case concerned. So to determine the probability of a couple having children take the age (in months) of the elder and subtract from it that of the younger. Divide by seven, and foretell, if the remainder is 1, 2, 3, 4, 5, or 6, a positive outlook. But if there is no remainder the portent is negative. It is a system that can rarely fail.[7]

Once pregnant, the desire is to know whether a boy or a girl is to be expected. So write down the mystic number 49 (seven sevens), add the number of months since conception, and subtract the age of the mother from the total. From this subtract 1, then 2, and so on up to 9, as long as this is possible. If the remainder is odd —a boy, if even—a girl. Here the interpretation is perhaps influenced by the Chinese odd = *yang*, male; even = *yin*, female.[8]

The child is born and some time after the excitement has died down, and the religious rites have been carried out,[9] the parents begin to wonder whether the child will be easy or hard to rear. So refer once more to the appropriate treatise. This tells one to add the year(s), months and days of age, and then multiply by the time of birth. Divide the total by eight. If the remainder is 1, 3, 5 or 7 the child will be hard to rear, but even numbers portend that it will be easy. If, alas, there is no remainder, soon there may be no child.[10]

Besides the infant there is another presence at a birth which requires attention, and that is the placenta or afterbirth. This is in accordance with a widespread belief that the way the placenta is treated presages good or bad consequences for the child.[11] Some would think it important enough to call in a soothsayer to choose the exact spot and depth at which the placenta should be buried; others nowadays would risk neglecting the whole matter, especially if no ground is available. However the treatise is fairly explicit: For children born in the 4th, 5th and 6th months burial of the placenta to the north of the house will be favourable. If born in the 7th, 8th or 9th month it should be buried to the north or north-east, but not to the east, for in that case the child would be hard to rear. If the birth is in the 10th, 11th or 12th month, the placenta should be buried to the south or north-east with good results. If the child is born in the 1st, 2nd or 3rd month it will live long, provided that the placenta is buried to the south or south-east.

The choice of a lucky monosyllabic name, which will later be replaced by a more permanent one corresponding to our Christian name, is a help towards bringing up the child successfully. The treatises list appropriate names, depending on the day of birth and sex, such as *lè* for a boy and *kèo* for a girl born on Sunday, *wan* for a boy and *lék* for a girl born on Monday, etc.[12]

Such is the trust in the power of the planets that the parents can get an idea straightaway as to what is the approximate outlook for a child born on any particular day of the week. In a nutshell it summarizes the lighthearted optimistic Thai view of life which may not exactly be a bed of roses but in which for most people things might be expected to turn out well enough in the end. The original is written in rather rough verse, of which the following will give the gist:

Sunday. A carefree person working ineffectually and about as much help to others as fire is to water. Will have the advantage of a powerful patron.[13] Will be a good conversationalist. Will be trustworthy, generous and faithful to friends. Very ready to settle in a dispute and if has done wrong will make amends. Will be poor when young but later will become well-off. Will then like to show off and will possess many wives. His knowledge of the world will be an asset.[14]

Monday. He is likely to be home-loving when young, but grows up to be fearless and proud, seeking then to associate with persons of high station. Though kindly-spoken he will be hard-hearted and apt to leave home. Then he is likely to develop a physical defect or some disease from which he will suffer severely. He may fall to low estate through the fault of others. Eventually he will be restored to a high position—and will die of dropsy.

Tuesday. A brave spirit, prone to quick anger and unyielding to others. Will be a strong support to parents and family but annoyed by some relatives. Intelligent, kindly spoken and active. Must move elsewhere to succeed. Trouble will come in two periods; but will achieve a prosperous and peaceful old age.

Wednesday. Will have a good disposition, but will lack the right sort of relatives to get him on. A careless person not troubling about past or future, and ready to depend on others where possible. As a monk he would be well thought of. But he will prefer to associate with ne'er-do-wells, and will be much loved by women. Tending thus to associate with the lower orders he will experience ups and downs in life.

Thursday. He will be good-natured but poor, and will have to leave home for a living. Later he will become sufficiently well-off and able to support himself. He will be trusted by his friends and will do good, though not liking to carry out his duties as a feudal client. Will be subject to lapses and have many wives. Likely to be engaged in law suits two or three times, but his wealthy friends will come to his aid, and he will end up happily.

Friday. He will be unfortunate at first, becoming an orphan with his father dying first, and when young will be badly treated by his relatives. A trustworthy character, he would make an ideal monk. After a period of trouble he should later become happy.

Saturday. A brave and proud spirit with many friends, but relatives will be likely to quarrel and make trouble for him. He will be pleasure loving and fond of the opposite sex, at the same time wishing to associate with important people. He is likely to be taken advantage of by relatives and others; and despite his courage he will never become rich.[15]

Some people believe that the day of birth indicates where the child spent his last life, the place from which he has just been reborn and this gives an indication of his future prospects: *Sunday:* Klinggaratha (South India), courageous, but sickly. *Monday:* Nāga domain, will be powerful. *Tuesday:* Tāpana (a hot hell), will be strong and helpful to rulers in war. *Wednesday:* Lankā (Ceylon), very intelligent. *Thursday:* Heaven, much merit and prosperity. *Friday:* Uttarakuru (mythical realm), mediocre. *Saturday:* Magadha (India), brave.[16]

NOTES TO CHAPTER I

1. *B* III, pp. 71–75. This divination myth bears some resemblances to the story of Kapila to be considered in Chapter X.
2. *Laws of Manu, Sacred Books of the East*, XXV, p. 39.
3. Cf. Dubois and Beauchamp, *Hindu Manners, Customs and Ceremonies*, 3rd. edn., Oxford, 1928, pp. 237–240.
4. *Śatapatha Brāhmana*, SBE XII, p. 10.
5. This protective *devatā* does not seem to be the same as the *khvăn̄*, or butterfly spirit, believed by the Thai to reside in the head. It suggests rather the Burmese 'centre of vigour' believed to move downwards from the head towards the toes, not however during the day but throughout the week. (Hastings' *Encyclopaedia*, Vol. III, art. Burma, p. 29) Or the *rāṣī*, 'beauty' of the Thai which moves similarly (*B* II, p. 81.).
6. *B* I, pp. 92 f. And briefly referred to by A. Bastian, *Reisen in Siam*, Jena, 1867, p. 492.
7. *B* I, p. 56.
8. However the remainders method, as popularly employed, is probably derived from traditional Thai astrology (cf. Zoro, *Gu mū'horà Thai to'm: cakradīpanī sarigrau*, Bangkok, 1965, Chapter 10). It has a place in some Indian astrological systems: see B.V. Raman, *Ashtakavarga system of prediction*, Bangalore, 1977.
9. H. G. Quaritch Wales, 'Siamese Theory and Ritual connected with pregnancy, birth and infancy', *Journ. Royal Anthrop. Inst.*, Vol. LXIII, 1933, pp. 441–451.
10. *B* I, p. 57.
11. See J. G. Frazer, *The Golden Bough*, abridged edn., 1949, pp. 39–41.
12. *B* I, p.58. The choice of a more permanent name also depends on day of birth and sex (see *BSMB*, pp. 249–260).
13. This refers to the Thai feudal system which was abolished only towards the end of last century. Every freeman or client had to attach himself to some patron, who in return for some personal service afforded him some protection; and much of this traditional attitude still persists in the relations of employees to employers. For a full study of the Thai feudal system see my *Ancient Siamese Government and Administration*, London, 1934; repr. New York, 1965.
14. While this first set of prognostications theoretically is the same for both sexes, it is couched in terms that would apply mainly to boys.
15. *B* I, p. 37. Such infant classification, based merely on the week day of birth, may seem to be an over-simplification, but in this the Thai are not alone. Perhaps the reader will recall:
    > Monday's child is fair of face,
    > Tuesday's child is full of grace,
    > Wednesday's child is full of woe,
    > Thursday's child has far to go, *etc.*
16. *B* I, p. 41.

CHAPTER II
LIFE'S PROMISE
Fate Calculation

It cannot be long before the parents wish to know more definitely what the future holds for the newly-born. For the great majority who do not call in an astrologer, this means recourse to one or more popular systems of fortune-telling. The one I shall consider first is basically the 'fate calculation' (*thui ming*) of the Chinese. It may well have been known to the Thai at least since the thirteenth century A.D., by which time they had adopted the Chinese duodenary animal-year cycle. Of course it shows signs of naturalization, and of Indian influence. It has been made palatable to the Thai Hīnayāna Buddhists by the fact that every year in the cycle has become associated with some famous occurrence in one of the Jātakas (Birth Stories).[1] Then again prognostications are left vague, intentionally it would seem, especially in regard to the days, so as to leave room for the soothsayer to exercise the psychological skill on which his reputation largely depends. This is borne out by a Cambodian manuscript, in the possession of the Musée Guimet, Paris, which, though well-illustrated, appears very incomplete by Thai standards. It was probably never intended as more than a soothsayers' *aide-mémoire*, as is remarked by its translator.[2]

In the Thai texts,[3] at the head of each year a specific being is illustrated riding on the animal of the year and accompanied by a particular tree (Plates I and II). In this another spirit, the *khvăñ* spirit of the year, is held to reside. The latter appears to represent the fortunes of the people in a generalized way, while at the same time each person has his individualized *khvăñ* resident in his head. This would point to a Chinese or more ancient Mongolian origin for this primitive animistic Thai conception which has puzzled many writers on Siam. Apart from the above-mentioned representations, the only other illustrations in this type of manuscript are usually figures of the animal intended to convey his character and fate during each quarter of the year.

Basic to the Chinese system of fate calculation are the five elements: wood, fire, earth, metal and water. These being divided into antitheses (active-passive, male-female) give the sub-cycle of the ten heavenly stems (e.g. growing wood, building wood, natural fire, artificial fire), while a second sub-cycle forms the twelve earthly branches or animal cycle. By combining with the day, month and year of birth the fate calculators arrived at their conclusions.[4] However here Indian influence asserts itself, for the Chinese did not recognize the months as divided into weeks, with week-days named after the planets. But the Thai had adopted the Indian week so here the days are named after the planets, though in the present system of divination the character of the day is entirely that of the year animal. The Brahmanical influence asserts itself more strongly in the first section of the prognostics for each year. Then the Hindu concept of the individual being a microcosm seems to have been superimposed on the original animal interpretation preserved in the month and day portents. Thus in this first section the prognostics relate the planets to five parts of the human body–mouth, heart, loins, hands and feet, and the characteristics are more such as would be derived from a reflection of the qualities of planetary deities. However, this is immediately followed by a sentence or two giving a tersely mundane statement of the fortunes to be expected.

Next, there follows a section dealing with the birth months, in quarterly divisions, in which the type of the particular animal is defined, in relation to the variety of the element by which it is governed. The human consequences are then briefly noted. Coming to the days, we find a rather more definite statement as to the lot or character of the animal, and equally so of the person born on that day. We are now in a position to face what fate has in store, as millions of Thai parents have done and still do.

Year of the Rat

A male *devatā* rides the Rat, and the element is water. The *khvăn* spirit resides in coconut or banana trees. It was in this year that in the *Temiya Jātaka* (as all Thai would know) the charioteer was about to bury the Bodhisattva Temiya.

Sun is the mouth: not afraid to talk to officials. Mars is the heart: rather inconstant, and satisfied with mediocre learning. Jupiter is the loins: strong sensuous desires. Moon and Mercury are the hands: hard-working but unskilful. Venus and Saturn are the feet: will like travel. When young, the child will be abandoned by relatives, and must depend on others. Later, however, will prosper. Will do government work well, assisting patron and becoming an official. Inclined to be harsh to wife and children. Desires wealth and appreciates culinary delicacies, but likes to associate with Brahmans[5] and is generous to the poor. If a woman, will have two sons on whom to depend. In infancy unhealthy and hard to rear. Having left home at fifteen will prosper elsewhere. Will have misfortunes at the ages of 11, 12, 16 and 31.

Born in the 5th, 6th or 7th months: the Rat is a white-bellied one and sea water is his element. He holds a crystal in his jaws and this means prosperity. 8th, 9th or 10th month: a long-snouted Rat, calm water. Good hearted though not a trustworthy speaker. 11th, 12th or 1st month: ghost Rat, jungle-water. A brave disposition but will find it hard to make a living. 2nd, 3rd or 4th month: big Field Rat, canal-water. A dim rat. Benevolent and will have many children.

Born on Sunday: will have much grief, but will be able to bear it. Monday, Thursday, Friday and Saturday: very good days. Tuesday and Wednesday: trouble. Except for Monday and Wednesday the days are associated with events in the career of Phya Sattalung, king of Cakravat and a friend of the demon king Rāvana, in the *Rāmakien* (Thai version of the Indian epic *Rāmāyana*).

Year of the Ox

A man rides the Ox, and the element is earth. The *khvăñ* lives in sugar palm. The Jātaka reference is to the occasion when Mahājānaka was rescued by Manimekhala.

Moon is the mouth: it is proud and speaks sharply, discussing arts and legal matters well. Mercury is the heart, which is clever in legal matters, and likes to associate with monks and nobles. Saturn is the loins: enjoying sensual pleasures. If a man, will have many wives; if a woman, inclined to secret affairs. Sun and Jupiter are the hands: craft ability very mediocre. Mars and Venus are the feet: not very suited for travel. If a trader, will be successful; and will have four sons, one powerful and one an official.

Born in 5th, 6th or 7th month: Wild Ox, sweet earth. A noble bull of good breeding, but difficult to use. Cruel, though good when young. 8th, 9th or 10th month: Plough Ox, element mud. Taciturn and brave. 11th, 12th or 1st month: a lame Ox, element mountain-top earth. It lives in the shed. Of good disposition, but difficult to make a living. 2nd, 3rd or 4th month: King of the Oxen, excellent earth. A puller, perfect in every respect, and very wealthy.

Born on Sunday: a bad-spirited Ox, not good. Monday: an excellent Ox. Very good and will have many attendants. Tuesday: a common Ox, not good. Wednesday: a broken-legged, blind Ox. Hard to rear. Thursday: an Ox of good disposition—will be wealthy. Friday: a pack Ox—must work hard and become very tired. Saturday: robbers steal this Ox, in order to kill it. Portends trouble.

Year of the Tiger

A *yakṣī* (female demon) rides the Tiger, and the element is wood. The *khvǎñ* lives in *Shorea* and *Hopea* or Rang *(Pentacma siamensis)*. Reference is to the *Sāma Jātaka* when Sāma went to draw water accompanied by the deer.

Mars is the mouth: liking to tell scurrilous stories about women. Jupiter is the heart: not very clever, having poor learning ability, but suitable to be a monk. Sun is the loins: will like sensuous pleasures. Mercury and Venus are the hands: craft ability good. Saturn and Moon are the feet: will travel much and be fortunate. This person will have a miserable youth, for cannot love relatives, but only others. At age two will have a misfortune, but at twenty will become flourishing and afterwards rich and powerful.

Born in the 5th, 6th or 7th month: Royal Tiger, dry wood. A watchful tiger. Very reliable, but will be in danger of becoming poor. 8th, 9th or 10th month: Fish Tiger, heart wood. Will have agreeable wives, sons and be wealthy. 11th, 12th or 1st month: Leopard, scented wood, reliable, wealthy. 2nd, 3rd or 4th month: a yellow man-eating Tiger, mountain tree wood. A very cunning type.

Born on Sunday: Tiger in a cave, difficult to find food. Monday: Tiger in a trap; much trouble likely. Tuesday: Tiger eats a man. Suggests an inclination to anger and ferocity. Wednesday: Tiger fasts; a good disposition. Excellent portent. Thursday: a Tiger reared by a holy hermit. A great future. Friday: Tiger falls over a precipice. Much trouble. Saturday: Tiger as a protective spirit, very good.

Year of the Hare

A woman-spirit rides the Hare, and the element is wood. The *khvǎñ* lives in the coconut and silk-cotton trees. Reference is to the *Nemi Jātaka*, when Nemi visits heaven and hell.

Mercury is the mouth, which is miserable and cannot speak pleasantly. Venus is the heart: audacious and desirous of helping the nobles. Unfortunately will be physically too weak to maintain self, but will be beloved by some. Moon is the loins: little sensuous desire, and no wish for concubines. Jupiter and Saturn are the hands: skilful at craftsmanship. Sun and Mars are the feet: will like travel. At the ages of 11, 12 and 15 will have trouble; and owing to physical weakness will probably suffer from sores on the face and some stomach trouble. However, will have slaves[6] and sufficient wealth. If goes in for agriculture should get good results. Will have one son for support.

Born in the 5th, 6th or 7th month: the Hare lives in the moon,[7] element dry wood. If poor will be free, and if good, prosperous. 8th, 9th or 10th month: Hare blind and broken-legged, element heart wood. Will be famous. 11th, 12th or 1st month: a lame Hare, element scented wood. Apt to be poor and suffer in hands and feet; but will do well later. 2nd, 3rd or 4th month: Hare has a bad fall, element hill-top wood. Will be cunning.

Born on Sunday: Hare flees fire. Trouble to be expected. Monday: Hare reared by a *devatā*; very good. Tuesday: a common Hare. Outlook miserable. Wednesday: a broken-legged Hare. Troubled outlook, with food supply difficult. Thursday: a Hare that runs quickly before its young. A quick-tempered person. Friday: a Hare with many attendants. A great future. Saturday: a Hare brought up by a lord. Wealthy, excellent prospects.

Year of the Large Snake (or Dragon)

A male *devatā* rides the Large Snake, and the element is metal (gold). The *khvǎñ* lives in the silk-cotton tree and bamboos. Reference is to the *Mahosadha Jātaka* when Mahosadha explained the riddles.

Jupiter is the mouth: it speaks with sagacity, the real knowledge of the scholar. Saturn is the heart, which is quick to anger, but soon recovers; a good-hearted person. Mars is the loins: sensuous desires strong, and given to secret vice. Venus and Sun are the hands: they lack skill and so do coarse work. Moon and Mercury are the feet: would like travel. The person will have reliable sons, the second one particularly worthy. Also many relatives, much money and many servants, both male and female. From 15 to 19 likely to have to live away from home. At 30 will be very fortunate but will suffer misfortunes at 37 and 50.

Born in the 5th, 6th or 7th month: Serpent king, element starry firmament. Will do government work well and have many slaves No enemy can harm. 8th, 9th or 10th month: large shining Snake, element stained gold. Apt to be poor when young, but later will do well. 11th, 12th or 1st month: a forest Cobra, element white gold. Good-hearted and benevolent. 2nd, 3rd or 4th month: a shining Reed Snake, element pure gold. A reliable person, will do good government work and become a high official.

Born on Sunday: noble Snake. Many attendants; very good. Monday: a common Snake, outlook poor. Tuesday: a poisonous Snake, apt to be evil. Wednesday: a sad Snake, will have much trouble. Thursday: a magic (?) Snake. Not good, will go to prison. Friday: a killer Snake. Miserable portent. Saturday: guardian Snake; very good.

Year of the Small Snake

A man-spirit rides the Small Snake, and the element is fire. The *khvăñ* lives in bamboos or Rang trees. Reference is to the *Bhuridatta Jātaka*, at the time when Bhuridatta lived coiled round the white ant-hill.

Venus is the mouth: kindly spoken but apt to be adulterous. Sun is the heart: likely to tell lies; not reliable. Mercury is the loins: will have enough carnal desire. Saturn and Moon are the hands: quick workers. Mars and Jupiter are the feet: will like travel. The individual should prosper but at 56 will have a misfortune.

Born in 5th, 6th or 7th month: lord Snake, element lightning. Probably a good person. 8th, 9th or 10th month: quick-eyed Cobra, element slow fire. Hard-hearted and very intelligent. 11th, 12th or 1st month: *Lai sap* Snake, element fire in stone. Good-hearted and kindly disposed. 2nd, 3rd or 4th month: green Snake, element fire in crystal. Good-hearted and will be successful. Born on Sunday: Snake flees fire and enters water. Trouble likely. Monday: Snake ensconced in a hole. Happy and trouble-free. Tuesday: Snake flees forest fire. Poor and troubled. Wednesday: common Snake. Difficult to rear; unfavourable. Thursday: guardian Snake, living in a golden cave. Lucky and will succeed. Friday: Snake guarding riches. A wealthy miser. Saturday: adulterous Snake. Man or woman will have illicit relations.

Year of the Horse (Plate I)

A female *devatā* rides the Horse, the element is fire and the *khvǎñ* lives in *Hopea* or banana. In the *Candakumāra Jātaka* it was in this year that the prince was helped by the *devas* at the sacrifice.

Saturn is the mouth, which likes to speak kindly. Moon is the heart: it wants to aim high. Jupiter is the loins: the indication is for constancy. Sun and Mars are the hands: not very skilled worker. Mercury and Venus are the feet: not given to much travel. When young will be beloved by parents. Between 21 and 25 will have to leave home in order to make a living. At 31 and 63 will suffer misfortunes.

Born in 5th, 6th or 7th month: king of Horses, element lightning. Will be intelligent and good-natured. 8th, 9th or 10th month: unfortunate Horse, element slow fire. If a woman, will be vagrant and a scandal-monger. 11th, 12th or 1st month: domestic Horse, fire in stone. Will never be wealthy. 2nd, 3rd or 4th month: a lame Horse, element fire in crystal. Will achieve high rank and be wealthy.

Born on Sunday: a noble Horse. Will have much power. Monday: a Horse cared for by a *devatā*. Fortunate and successful. Tuesday: a Horse reared by a warrior. Will be wealthy. Wednesday: common and badly-behaved Horse. Unfortunate. Thursday: a noble's Horse; rich but very tired. Friday: this Horse's mother died. Miserable, without shelter. Saturday: a Horse with damaged nerves or muscles; troubled outlook.

Year of the Goat

A female *devatā* rides the Goat, the element is metal (gold) and the *khvǎñ* lives in the Pārijāta (mythical) Tree and short-jointed bamboo. Here the association is with the *Nārada Jātaka* when the

Bodhisattva as the great Brahmā-deva descended to earth carrying gold.
Sun is the mouth, which speaks agreeably to the lords. Mars is the heart, which likes to obtain enough knowledge for self-satisfaction. Not treating family well and only interested in wealth. Venus is the loins: carnal desires strong. Moon and Mercury are the hands: though lacking skill they work diligently. Jupiter and Saturn are the fee: will travel much. Will lack relatives when young, and at one be hard to rear, suffering misfortunes at 11 and 12. At 15 will go away to seek a living and will be lucky, though there will be more misfortunes at 16 and 31. If the individual takes up government employment, will do well, and will get on well with the Brahmans. Will have the support of two sons.

Born in 5th, 6th or 7th month: the Goat, element sky-gold, has difficulty in finding food. Likes learning as an aid to self, but can never become rich. 8th, 9th or 10th month: domestic Goat, element stained gold. Likely to experience sorrow and trouble. 11th, 12th or 1st month: a lame Goat, likely to suffer in the hands and feet; but of a military bent, very intelligent and will do well. 2nd, 3rd or 4th month: a lord rears this Goat, whose element is fine gold. Of a good and kindly disposition, will become great and rich.

Born on Sunday: market-place Goat—not successful. Monday: Goat kept by a noble. Will be rich —very good. Tuesday: Goat kept by blind person; will lack the necessities of life. Wednesday: Goat brought up by a great teacher. Will be very intelligent; very good. Thursday: Goat kept by an august personage. Will be successful. Friday: poor Goat, unable to find food or support. Saturday: blind Goat—much trouble.

Year of the Monkey (Plate II)

A *yakṣa* (demon) rides the Monkey, the element being metal (iron) while the *khvǎñ* lives in the Jack tree. Reference is to the *Vidhura Jātaka*, when Vidhura, tied to the *yakṣa's* horse's tail, visited the Nāga kingdom.

Moon is the mouth, which speaks with knowledge and is always striving to learn; agreeable to monks and nobles. Mercury is the heart: well suited for litigation. Saturn is the loins: strongly sensuous, liking women's company and apt to have a plurality of wives. If a woman, probably addicted to vice. Mars and Jupiter are the hands: not without skill, but a slow worker. Venus and Sun are the feet: not wishing to travel. If a trader, will succeed. Will have the support of four sons, one of them an official.

Born in 5th, 6th or 7th month: an excellent Monkey, element soft iron. A mild disposition, not very helpful to others, but will develop. 8th, 9th or 10th month: forest Monkey, element alluvial iron. Faithful and good; will succeed. 11th, 12th or 1st month: Monkey of the mangroves, element good iron. Of a military disposition, will have many servants and slaves. 2nd, 3rd or 4th month: wind Monkey, element purified iron. Hard to rear, but will have a good disposition and repute.

Born on Sunday: a Monkey reared by a lord; very good. Monday: a common Monkey, likely to be poor; not good. Tuesday: an imprisoned Monkey. Misfortune and troubles indicated. Wednesday: Monkey reared by a hermit; well informed, very good. Thursday: Monkey brought up by a chief Brahman. Intelligent, clever. Friday: an excellent Monkey. Very fortunate. Saturday: a chained Monkey. Will probably suffer. Not good.

Year of the Cock

A *yakṣa* rides the Cock and the element is metal (iron). The *khvăñ* lives in the *Dipterocarpus* or in the silk-cotton tree. Reference is to the *Vessantara Jātaka*, when with his wife and child the Bodhisattva left for Mount Vamka.

Mars is the mouth, liking to tell risky stories about women. Jupiter is the heart: not very prudent or with good memory, but good-hearted and law-abiding. Sun is the loins: strong carnal desires. Mercury and Venus are the hands: skilful and able craftsmanship. Saturn and Moon are the feet: will like travel. Of poor parentage but later fortunate, though not able to be much help to others. From the age of 20 will concentrate on establishing own independence.

Born in 5th, 6th or 7th month: a village Cock, element soft iron. When young—poor, mild-natured and kindly. If a woman will probably remain a spinster. 8th, 9th or 10th month: a wild Cock, element alluvial iron. Good and intelligent, but sharp-tempered. 11th, 12th or 1st month: an aimlessly wandering Cock, element good iron. Cannot acquire reason and is likely to get into trouble. Nevertheless good at heart. 2nd, 3rd or 4th month: an excellent Cock, element purified iron. Wealthy and intelligent, liking to acquire knowledge. Very good portent.

Born on Sunday: a Cock brought up in comfort by a noble. Very good. Monday: this Cock cannot find food. Poverty and trouble to be expected. Tuesday: a Game Cock. Likely to be a ne'er-do-well or gamester. Wednesday: Cock kept by a chief Brahman. Clever and learned. Very good. Thursday: Cock kept by a fine person. Good fortune. Friday: a bad Cock. Trouble indicated, not good. Saturday: Cock reared by a Brahman. Wealthy, very good.

Year of the Dog

A *yakṣī* rides the Dog, and the element is earth. The *khvăñ* lives in *Sterculia foetida* or in royal lotus. There is a reference to the *Sutasoma Jātaka*.

Mercury is the mouth, which cannot speak pleasantly, except to serve its own ends. Venus is the heart: brave-spirited and would like to serve the rulers, enjoying scenes of battle, but will be handicapped by bodily weakness. Moon is the loins: weak sensuous desires. Jupiter and Saturn are the hands: skilful and expert in crafts. Sun and Mars are the feet: no desire for travel. Liable to facial sores and to indigestion. Will have adequate wealth and enough slaves. Garden cultivation would be profitable. Will have one son as a support. Misfortunes likely in 11th, 13th and 25th years.

Born in 5th, 6th or 7th month: domestic Dog, element sweet earth. Unfortunate when young, but will succeed later. 8th, 9th or 10th month: sporting Dog, with an owner, element mud. Faithful, fortunate and very intelligent. 11th, 12th or 1st month: Fox, element mountain-top earth. Clever, and of combative spirit. 2nd, 3rd or 4th month: market-place Dog, element clay (for wattle). Possessed of a combative spirit; will be able to maintain self.

Born on Sunday: hunting Dog, must work and get tired. Monday: hermit's Dog. Good ability and knowledge. Tuesday: mangy Dog. Miserable and hard to find food. Wednesday: well-attended Dog. Rich, very good. Thursday: mad Dog. Speaks angrily and is of evil disposition. Friday: Dog reared by a noble. Will be wealthy. Saturday: Dog that must be chained. If male, a ne'er-do-well.

Year of the Pig

A woman rides the Pig, and the element is water. The *khvăñ* resides in lotus plants of two kinds. Reference is to the *Suphamitra Jātaka*.

Jupiter is the mouth, which speaks with knowledge, but is not always trustworthy. Saturn is the heart: hot-tempered but quickly recovering and not vengeful. Mars is the loins: liable to carnal faults; if a man will seek the wives of others. Venus and Sun are the hands: if must work will get tired. Moon and Mercury are the feet: will like travel. At 19 will leave home, and will have two sons, the second being good. Will have many friends, much wealth and many slaves.

Born in 5th, 6th or 7th month: this Pig is kept by a lord, its element is sea-water. Will have merit and much intelligence. 8th, 9th or 10th month: Pig kept in a sty, element calm water. Good and very faithful. 11th, 12th or 1st month: a leprous Pig, element jungle water. Goodhearted and reliable. 2nd, 3rd or 4th month: a wild Pig, holding a crystal in its jaws. Element canal-water. Good-hearted. Very good portent.

Born on Sunday: Pig reared by a noble. Fortunate and prosperous. Monday: Pig killed for eating. Sorrow and trouble foretold. Tuesday: a rich man's Pig. Wealthy. Wednesday: a common Pig. Poor, not good. Thursday: a hill Pig. Will like wandering (for pleasure). Friday: a Pig with a bad head and broken leg. Trouble forecast. Saturday: a well-attended Pig. Excellent outlook.

On the above a few generalizations suggest themselves. With whatever planet a part of the 'microcosm' begins, Sun in the case of mouth, the order follows the days of the week throughout the twelve year cycle. There is one exception where Saturn replaces Venus in the case of the loins of Ox. Furthermore, approximately the same character is given to the same planet when it repeats later in the cycle. Adaptation to Thai society is indicated by the evident acceptance of the principle that it is open to any freeman to achieve any position fate may decree, and that high official or noble is considered preferable to success in trade.[8] When the year animal is domestic the care or lack of it afforded by the owner is significant for in human society this is reflected in the generosity of the feudal patron—nowadays of the employer. The Buddhist monks

LIFE'S PROMISE

are of course highly respected, but in our texts even more so the Brahmans, these latter a hold-over from the Ayudhyā period when they were a much more influential section of society. Finally, we cannot fail to note that the portent for the month of birth can often be virtually the opposite of that for the day. And that is just what appeals to the Thai temperament, enabling one to be set off against the other, leaving a favourable balance of course.

A simple numerical alternative

Despite the time-honoured authority of 'fate calculation' as above described, a simpler system has won wide popular appeal. And this popularity is clearly shown by the wealth of indigenous-style illustration with which it is accompanied in the manuscripts. In this system the twelve-year animal-cycle has only a calendrical significance, reliance being placed on the divinatory power of numbers—of ultimately astrological derivation.[9] So the months of each year of the cycle are considered in pairs, beginning with months 5 and 11, and accompanied by a day, or two days in the first case, in order to accommodate the odd seventh day. The inquirer must then find the prediction for both the month and the day of birth. An introductory note explains that if predictions for both month and day are good this is very good, if one is good and one bad take the mean, only if both are bad is the outlook indeed depressing. Such favourable odds are naturally encouraging to the curious. As to the illustrations I should mention that the first one for each year merely shows the year spirit riding the appropriate steed and perhaps accompanied by the *khvăn's* tree, just as previously. So I shall not mention these below. It is the subsequent illustrations that graphically depict the fate of lucky or unlucky individuals in traditional Thai manner.

Year of the Rat (Plate III)

Month 5 or 11, or day 1 or 7: will be intelligent and able to fend for self, but liable to quarrel over spouse. Month 6 or 12, or day 2: *devatā* in grand boat. Will be wealthy and travel widely. Trading by boat would be successful. Month 7 or 1, or day 3: poverty symbolized by a woman riding a cow. Will have trouble at least once, and much difficulty in gaining a living. Month 8 or 2, or day 4: a woman in a house. Will be wealthy as a result of someone's gifts. This is better for a woman, but not unsatisfactory for a man. Month 9 or 3, or day 5: couple pounding rice. Will be very poor and must work as hard as slaves. Month 10 or 4, or day 6: *devatā* riding *nāga*. Will have a severe disposition, liable to anger; will be powerful.

Year of the Ox (Plate IV)

Month 5 or 11, or day 1 or 7: will be adequately well-off, but of uncertain temperament, sometimes pleasant, sometimes the reverse. Month 6 or 12, or day 2: prisoner wearing a cangue collar. Will experience litigation and have much trouble. If a man the trouble comes from a woman, if a woman vice versa. Month 7 or 1, or day 3: man riding a fine horse. Will like travel rather than staying at home; would succeed in government service. Month 8 or 2, or day 4: husband and wife quarrelling. Will often speak aggressively, and so become engaged in altercations. Month 9 or 3, or day 5: youth riding a bull. When young will get into trouble, but when adult will do well, succeeding through own efforts. Month 10 or 4, or day 6: man riding a *nāga*. An active type who works very quickly. People likely to fear his ferocity.

Year of the Tiger (Plate V)

Month 5 or 11, or day 1 or 7: fierce and powerful, a terse speaker who keeps his word; but finds it hard to bring up his sons. Month 6 or 12, or day 2: man with attendant. Will be great, have many slaves and do good government work. Month 7 or 1, or day 3: woman riding a *nāga*. Hard-hearted and fierce, only liking amusement and apt to be diseased. Month 8 or 2, or day 4: man asleep in a palace. Will do well and be very happy. Will have so many attendants that never need feel tired. Month 9 or 3, or day 5: woman in house. Wealthy and happy. Month 10 or 4, or day 6: noble riding a *nāga*. Active disposition and position of power; but often worried by litigation.

Year of the Hare

Month 5 or 11, or day 1 or 7: happy and well-off. Month 6 or 12, or day 2: noble riding a fine horse. Great good fortune. Month

7 or 1, or day 3: man sitting in a boat paddled by a servant. Will have wealth and slaves and never feel tired. Month 8 or 2, or day 4: woman who, like Vessantara's wife, heads for the jungle. Sorrow and trouble indicated, owing to need to leave home and go elsewhere. Month 9 or 3, or day 5: two men fighting. Very quarrelsome and satisfied to be ne'er-do-well. Often in litigation, so troubled in mind; not at all good. Month 10 or 4, or day 6: man riding a *nāga*. A brave person who should do well in government service, though of poor health.

Year of the Large Snake

Month 5 or 11, or day 1 or 2: likely to get angry and not recover for a long time, but will do good government work. Month 6 or 12, or day 2: a noble seated on a dais. Will be great and enjoy continuing good fortune. Month 7 or 1, or day 3: a prisoner in chains. Will experience much sorrow and be worried by an enemy who meditates evil. But able to protect self. Month 8 or 2, or day 4: mahout riding elephant. A poor person, finding it hard to make a living. Month 9 or 3, or day 5: a noble riding a horse. Will be a wealthy noble; must often travel far afield. Month 10 or 4, or day 6: a noble riding *nāga*. Will do well, but though strong physically will have mental anxieties and little happiness.

Year of the Small Snake (Plate VI)

Month 5 or 11, or day 1 or 7: will be powerful and do good government work, but liable to fits of anger from which recovery is slow. Month 6 or 12, or day 2: a young man followed by umbrella-bearer. Fortunate from youth on, with parents to lean on, and many slaves. Month 7 or 1, or day 3: person wearing cangue. Will get into trouble and others will seek to harm. Or will be apt to suffer from fever. Not good. Month 8 or 2, or day 4: man seated on a throne, with umbrella-bearers and fan-wavers. Will be highly prosperous and enjoy all kinds of happiness. Month 9 or 3, or day 5: mahout riding elephant. Will be very poor and work till the sweat runs down, or must seek a better patron. Month 10 or 4, or day 6: man riding *nāga*. An active-minded person, firm and never accepting defeat. If in government service will do well.

Year of the Horse

Month 5 or 11, or day 1 or 7: a mild teacher, grateful to benefactor. Will do well enough to maintain self. Month 6 or 12, or day 2: mahout riding elephant. Will have difficulty making a living. Month 7 or 1, or day 3: husband and wife quarrelling. Very poor, and will find it hard to get a living. Apt to quarrel or to indulge in extra-marital relations. Month 8 or 2, or day 4: *devatā* riding a fine horse. Fortunate, but must travel a great deal. Month 9 or 3, or day 5: lord carried on a palanquin. Fortunate in every way. Month 10 or 4, or day 6: *devatā* riding a *nāga*. Quick-minded but apt to leave work uncompleted. Will be adequately well-off.

Year of the Goat

Month 5 or 11, or day 1 or 7: a good person, never angry. Likes to follow the right path; will be industrious and well-off. Month 6 or 12, or day 2: drunkards paddling a boat. Will be poor and tired, with difficulty in making a living. Month 7 or 1, or day 3: *devatā* riding a fine horse. Will be prosperous and have a tiring life, for in order to do well must travel afar. Month 8 or 2, or day 4: noble seated on a dais. Will be fortunate and rise higher than relatives. Much happiness. Month 9 or 3, or day 5: mahout riding elephant. Will be exhausted trying to attain rank; will never be happy. Month 10 or 4, or day 6: man riding *nāga*. A rash speaker, inviting litigation, and acts according to own conscience. But will attain rank.

Year of the Monkey (Plate VII)

Month 5 or 11, or day 1 or 7: does violence without fear of sinning: A bad worker and poorly-off; not good. Month 6 or 12, or day 2: a seated noble accompanied by umbrella- and fan-bearers. Will be lucky, have dignity and much happiness. Month 7 or 1, or day 3: two men fighting. Will have trouble, be wicked and find it hard to make a living. Month 8 or 2, or day 4: husband and wife quarrelling. Will be miserable and have sad married life, and will not stay long anywhere. Month 9 or 3, or day 5: woman riding an ox. Will be very tired, and dependent on others. Month 10 or 4, or day 6: *devatā* riding *nāga*. Active-minded, harsh-speaking, but will hold position of power.

Year of the Cock

Month 5 or 11, or day 1: angry and quarrelsome. Month 6 or 12, or day 2: man riding horse. Must travel much to gain a living. Would do government work well and gain rank. Month 7 or 1, or day 3: noble reclining on couch; very fortunate. Month 8 or 2, or day 4: young man riding a cow. Will have rank and position, but cannot find happiness. Likely to have to travel afar. Month 9 or 3, or day 5: woman carrying baskets. Will have trouble and little reward. Tired. Month 10 or 4, or day 6: *devatā* riding *nāga*. Will be daring and powerful, feared by all. Wealthy enough.

Year of the Dog (Plate VIII)

Month 5 or 11, or day 1 or 7: a fierce person, but brings up children well. Can make a living but will have marital trouble. Month 6 or 12, or day 2: man riding *nāga*. A quick-minded person who will have power. Will have wealth, but not contentment. Month 7 or 1, or day 3: noble on fine seat, with umbrella- and fan-bearers. Fortunate, great and prosperous. Month 8 or 2, or day 4: mahout riding elephant. Will like travel and depend on good patron, but will not be rich. Month 9 or 3, or day 5: young man riding horse. A quick worker and fast traveller. Will do good government work and attain rank. Month 10 or 4, or day 6: *devatā* seated on dais. Fortune, prosperity and happiness of all kinds.

Year of the Pig

Month 5 or 11, or day 1 or 7: a careless money-wasting person, not industrious and must depend on others. Also a busybody. Month 6 or 12, or day 2: noble reclining on couch. Will be great and prosperous. Month 7 or 1, or day 3: man paddled in fine boat. Will be a good person, fortunate and respected by all. Month 8 or 2, or day 4: man riding a cow. Will be tired, have difficulty in getting money, but able to get just enough. Month 9 or 3, or day 5: noble on fine seat, with umbrella- and fan-bearers. Lucky, wealthy and respected by all. Month 10 or 4, or day 6: *devatā* riding a *nāga*. An angry person, never calm.

In keeping with the accompanying illustrations, the adaptation to the Thai character and locale is more evident than in the previously described system. Thus there is little to support the Hindu microcosmic conception by which it is supposed that the planets may give the feet an itch to travel. On the contrary the ideal (by no means extinct today) seems to be the attainment of a comfortable government position with adequate wealth and servants. While leisure is highly prized, travel too often implies an unattractive post distant from the capital. Symbolically, carrying baskets, riding a cow or even an elephant (as mahout) suggest hard work and exhaustion. If one must travel, rather than sit or recline at home in cool comfort, then a fine boat or horse signify that it will be worth while; but for persons of a not very desirable temperament the *nāga* suggests itself as a suitable mount.

The Treatise of the Seven Numbers

We have now to consider a more sophisticated numerical system as explained in the manuscripts under this heading.[10] In this system reliance is placed entirely on the divinatory power of the seven numbers, ultimately planetary no doubt. The tables that follow may not make the most attractive form of literature, but I think that from them the reader can derive a deeper insight into the traditional preoccupations of the Thai people.

For the day of birth the week days are numbered 1 to 7, and for each there are seven classes of prediction, thus allowing of a greater differentiation of portents than we have seen hitherto. The seven classes are: personal, fortune, business sense, father, mother, wealth, social.[11] These terms should be considered as short labels, giving only a partial conception of the subject-matter of the prognostication. Now each day, according to its place in the week, numbers the classes accordingly, at the same time changing their character for better or worse. So for Sunday, personal is 1, for Monday 2 and so on. The complete series for Saturday is 7 1 2 3 4 5 6.

For the twelve months there is a similar series of seven classes of prediction: personal, prosperity, friends, children male, children female, enemies, spouse. But as there are more months than classes of prediction, while the sixth month starts with 6 and the seventh with 7, the others in pairs share a starting number, thus first and eighth months start with 1, second and ninth with 2 and so on. For the 5th and 12th month the series runs 5 6 7 1 2 3 4.

For the twelve years of the animal cycle there is a similar series again, of seven classes of prediction: death, patron (feudal, transferable to employer), fate (*kamma*), wealth, travel, private and state employment. As with the months, except with Small Snake which starts with 6 and Horse which starts with 7, all the years are paired, and as with the paired months we have no need to repeat the predictions.

Sunday. 1. Personal: when young will depend more on father than on mother, will be eloquent and self-reliant. 2. Fortune: will be a gambler, caring little for wealth. 3. Business sense: will be extravagant. 4, 5. Father, mother: mother will die first. 6. Wealth: generous to relatives. 7. Social: a bold conversationalist.

Monday. 2. Personal: when young will leave home and be brought up by an important Brahman. Later there will be a great man living to the north who will rear as own child, and help with money. But will not be helpful to others and will only speak agreeably to the influential. 3. Fortune: will not be wealthy at first. 4. Business sense: better not keep money oneself, but allow a trusted person to invest it. 5, 6. Father, mother: father will die first. 7. Wealth: will not be acquisitive. 1. Social: will associate with someone who is at first friendly, but later will quarrel; then will do a favour to the unfriendly person.

Tuesday. 3. Personal: mentally well-equipped and as cannot depend on friends must be completely self-reliant. 4. Fortune: will be wealthy and have all kinds of possessions. 5. Business sense: not good at looking after belongings. 6, 7. Father, mother: father will die first. 1. Wealth: will be well-off. 2. Social: speaks pleasantly and will seek a highly-respected patron.

Wednesday. 4. Personal: will have a broad face and thin hair, and do no good to anyone. Will speak well to one's face and the backbite. Many relatives, but no mother. 5. Fortune: will be wealthy. 6. Business sense: will guard wealth carefully. 7, 1. Father, mother: mother will die first. 2. Wealth: fond of money, but nevertheless generous. 3. Social: will travel and would like to make friends.

Thursday. 5. Personal: will speak well, with the intelligence and the knowledge of a learned man, but in fact would not wish to talk a great deal. Will have many children but would do government work well and please people. 6. Fortune: will possess much property. 7. Business sense: would not keep money, so should trust it to others to invest. 1, 2. Father, mother: father will die first. 3. Wealth: would be generous to those in want. 4. Social: would not wish to converse much, but would like to be well considered by all.

Friday. 6. Personal: will like women and have many wives. Will gain wealth through friends but may be slandered. 7. Fortune: will not keep wealth because will be a generous person who can refuse nobody. 1. Business sense: as cannot keep money must trust the investment of it to others. 2, 3. Father, mother: mother will die first. 4. Wealth: this will be made by own efforts. 5. Social: will not trust people, and will converse only with those with whom desires to have sexual relations.

Saturday. 7. Personal: owing to a birth defect may have the left eye damaged. Will talk affably to the great, but would do no one any good, talking agreeably to one's face and then backbiting. 1. Fortune: will fall heavily on one occasion. 2. Business sense: a miser. 3, 4. Father, mother: father will die first. 5. Wealth: will have wealth given by others. 6. Social: will speak gently and be agreeable only to the influential.

Months 1 and 8. 1. Personal: dark skin and slender form. 2. Prosperity: sufficiently well-off. 3. Friends: should associate with dark people. 4, 5. Children: should have a male child first. 6. Enemies: will have an enemy with yellow eyes and curly hair; if the enemy is a woman will have one breast pendant. 7. Spouse: will be bad and tell lies.

Months 2 and 9. 2. Personal: a fair person, then all will be well. 3. Prosperity: sufficiently well-off. 4. Friends: should associate with rather slender people. 5, 6. Children: male child first then all well. 7. Enemy: will have a dark enemy, but if a woman will be fair and tall. 1. Spouse: will have a good spouse on whom one can depend.

Months 3 and 10. 3. Personal: should be dark, then all well. 4. Prosperity: middling. 5. Friends: good outlook if associate with. fair persons. 6, 7. Children: will have brave, obedient children

LIFE'S PROMISE

1. Enemies: must beware of many enemies planning harm.
2. Spouse: will marry well, but will be likely to differ.

Months 4 and 11. 4. Personal: a fairish person. 5. Prosperity: will be a good person able to look after self. 6. Friends: associate with dark people, then all well. 7, 1. Children: boy first, then all well. 2. Enemy: a woman will meditate evil. 3. Spouse: rather fierce speaking, but means well.

Months 5 and 12. 5. Personal: Rather dark, but fortunate. 6. Prosperity: a good person who will succeed because of a helper. 7. Friends: if associate with dark robust people all will be well. 1, 2. Children: lucky if it is a girl first. 3. Enemy: will have an enemy with yellow eyes and curly hair. 4. Spouse: rather bold-speaking.

Month 6. 6. Personal: a fair, tall person, not very pleasant-speaking. 7. Prosperity: not well-off. 1. Friends: miserable and apt to grumble 2, 3. Children: boy first will be lucky. 4. Enemy: a dark person, probably with a sore, will plan harm. 5. Spouse: a good person who will encourage spouse to be strong in the faith (Buddhist, presumably).

Month 7. 7. Personal: will be a well-formed dark person. 1. Prosperity: middling, able to support self. 2. Friends: associate with dark people and all will be well. 3, 4. Children: a boy first will be good. 5. Enemy: a person with thin hair and yellow eyes. 6. Spouse: one who speaks well and can be trusted.

Years of the Rat (1) and the Goat (8). 1. Death: courageous but sad. 2. Patron: will speak agreeably so will be well received anywhere. 3. Fate: has demerit from former birth, and likes to talk about others. 4. Wealth: likely to be rich. 5. Travel: will probably travel, and make many friends. 6, 7. Employment: would succeed in government work, with the help of friends.

Years of the Ox (2) and the Monkey (9). 2. Death: likely to be separated from spouse. 3. Patron: will go where will be well received by a patron. 4. Fate: likes talking about others. 5. Wealth: will receive property from an important Brahman, or be helped by the latter to get it. 6. Travel: would travel quickly. 7, 1. Employment: not suitable to be an official, and in service of a patron will be liable to be punished for the misdeeds of others.

Years of the Tiger (3) and the Cock (10). 3. Death: when time comes will die because work is unsatisfactory. 4. Patron: will find a patron who will not treat well. 5. Fate: will suffer from rather bad demerit in a former life; will speak agreeably to one's face, but then backbite. 6. Wealth: will obtain gold. 7. Travel: if must travel, will be likely to get ill or become footsore. 1, 2. Employment: would serve a patron well and do good official work, in the latter case because of the help of a fair person.

Years of the Hare (4) and the Dog (11). 4. Death: when time comes, will die of poison. 5. Patron: will look far and wide for a patron, and be received by a distant one. 6. Fate: will have great learning, resulting from merit acquired in a former life. 7. Wealth: will have much silver and gold: but also an angry nature. 1. Travel: a speedy traveller, but only safe if accompanied by a friend. 2, 3. Employment: will have a good patron because a woman helps; but would make a poor official.

Years of the Large Snake (5) and the Pig (12). 5. Death: will die on patron's behalf. 6. Patron: will look for a patron who will love one as a relative. 7. Fate: has demerit from a former life, and so will suffer because of others. 1. Wealth: will obtain wealth from a woman. 2. Travel: a slow walker, who should take great care. 3, 4. Employment: would do well for a patron; as an official would become celebrated.

Year of the Small Snake (6) 6. Death: will die exhausted, on behalf of a great man. 7. Patron: miserable, because the patron he seeks does not want him. 1. Fate: unable to help others. 2. Wealth: will obtain money from a young girl. 4. Travel: will travel afar, and talk about it. 4, 5. Employment: likely to serve a patron of only middling rank; not suitable for official work.

Year of the Horse (7). 7. Death: when time comes will die because of wealth. 1. Patron: will seek a patron who will treat as a relative, preferably a wealthy lord. 2. Fate: will suffer from the demerit of previous life. 3. Wealth: will have property that is liable to be damaged. 4. Travel: if travelling will be likely to fall behind. 5. 6. Employment: would serve a good patron well with the help of a *pandit;* or would do excellent official work.

Now a querent wishing to arrive at the destiny of any child of known birth day, month and year, in the light of the above indications, should tablulate the position in 'three tiers' as in Fig 1, supposing that in this example the birth was on the second day of the fifth month of the eighth year of the animal cycle.

Day	Personal	Fortune	Business sense	Father/Mother		Wealth	Social	
2	2	3	4	5	6	7	1	
Month	Personal	Prosperity	Friends	Children		Enemy	Spouse	
5	5	6	7	1	2	3	4	
Year	Death	Patron	Fate	Wealth		Travel	Employment	
8	1	2	3	4		5	6	7

Fig. 1

He will then make what he can of the portents by combining the relevant indications. But the soothsayers have realized that life is not so simple as that. They have noted that the prognostications fall into four groups, more or less favourable. Considered favourable are: business sense, wealth (day and year), and patron. Unfavourable: fortune, enemies, death, fate and travel. Less favourable: employment and prosperity. Neutral: social. So the inquirer must then proceed to observe whether the personal numbers are the same as any of the other numbers, for the outlook will thereby be modified.

In the example given in Fig. 1 personal (day) 2, being the same as one of the children numbers, stands for many progeny who will resemble their parent. But personal 2 is also the same number as patron, which ensures that the individual will be correct in demeanour, will be trustworthy, highly respected and prosperous. Now the personal (month) number is 5 and this happens to be the same as the number for travel, considered an unfavourable occupation. This unfortunately denotes a liability to suffer from illness or be troubled by oppression and appear sickly. One should then take business sense, of which the number in this example is 4, and it happens to be particularly lucky, coinciding with that of spouse and of wealth (year). This is interpreted as meaning that the person will both have a wealthy wife and also gain wealth through any work undertaken proving profitable. Then the coincidence of wealth.

(day) 7 with state employment is held to indicate a sufficiency of property.

It would be superfluous to enter further into the deductions to be drawn from the coincidences which the treatise tabulates minutely. Sufficient to say that, as in the example given, the logic exhibited does not always strictly follow what might be expected, though it thus may be more comforting to the parents! A prediction made better or worse by a coincidence of numbers would be annulled by a contrary prediction having the same number. Thus if business sense was the same number as enemy, loss and danger would be the portent, but this would in turn be annulled if patron also had the same number.

The obvious application of the microcosm to the three-tier system of predictions is of interest in connection with what we have already seen of such development. It is set up as in Fig. 2.

	HAND		MOUTH		HAND	
Day	Personal Fortune	Business sense	Father/Mother		Wealth	Social
	0	0	0	0	0	0
			HEART			
Month	Personal	Prosperity	Friends	Children	Enemy	Spouse
				male female		
	0	0	0	0 0	0	0
Year	Death	Patron	Fate	Wealth	Travel	Employment
	0	0	0	0	0	0
		FOOT		LOINS	FOOT	

Fig. 2

Number falling to   *Prognostication*
                                                     (as numbered)

        MOUTH (Father)

1. Speaks little, but wife will be a babbler.
2. Speaks agreeably, especially to lords and the aged.
3. A proud and boastful speaker.
4. At first speaks as a believer, later not so.
5. A gentle and elegant speaker.
6. Less likely to believe others than to blame them.
7. Will speak precisely, thinking first. If angry, very angry.

        HEART (Male children)

1. Will choose the life of a ne'er-do-well, spending money and a prey to emotions.

2. Not affable or constant, soon tiring of associates.
3. Brave, and would make a good official.
4. Kind-hearted and generous.
5. Obedient to parents and teachers; will be learned.
6. No consideration for others; if angry, will remain so.
7. Would make either a good official or a support to patron.

LOINS (Wealth)

1. Will have secret disease, unhappy marriage and, if a man, will have three wives.
2. Will love inconstantly and, if a man, will be adulterous.
3. (missing).
4. 5, 6. Happy and untroubled.
7. Secret intrigues; if a man, will have many wives and will not be content to live in one place.

HANDS (Spouse)

1. Wife will be a small, darkish woman, living to the N.W. or S.E.
2. Wife will be a thin fair woman, living to the south or east.
3. Wife will be an orphan but said to be very charming. She lives to the N.E. or S.W.
4. Wife will be young, fair, handsome and kind, but an orphan. She lives directly to the north or south.
5. Wife will be a widow, but young, living directly to the north or south.
6. Wife will be young, pretty but tall, and living to the west or east.
7. Wife will be a widow, or elderly, of dark complexion and sagging bust, but knowledgeable. She lives to the S.E. or N.W.

FEET (Female children)

1. or 3. If a boy is born first, he will be hard to rear.
5. Will have children on whom one can depend.
2. 4, 6. Female children will be first born, on whom one can depend.

The selection of spouse and female children as Hands and Feet does not fit the scheme well, but is evidently necessary owing to their being the only human agents available.

The seven numbers in five tiers

The seven numbers also lend themselves to divination by the remainder method, for which five tiers must be established.[12] One first writes the numbers for day, month and year of birth as previously.

Then you total the first column, take seven from it and if the total is still more than seven subtract seven again. Similarly with the other columns so that you can write a fourth tier, each figure of which is according to whatever is the remainder. Then call the numbers of this tier by the following portentous terms: *atma, dāsā, siddhijoga, bhogsompatī, mahācora, mahāupaśana, mahāupathamba*. Now make a fifth tier: take the total of the numbers of the four tiers, subtract seven, so that the total is not more than seven. Then write them beneath the fourth tier, and distinguish the numbers of this fifth tier as follows: personal, friends, relatives, wealth, property, boats, spouse.

If now you wish to know anyone's personal future, look at personal, and see what number of the fourth tier coincides with it. Similarly with the other matters. If *atma* coincides the effect is neutral; if *dāsā* does, then worse rather than better, if *siddhijoga* does, very good; if *bhogsompatī* does, there will be plenty; if *mahācora* does, property will be lost; if *mahāupaśana* does, dangers will be encountered; if *mahāupathamba* does, wealth will be gained.

The so-called 'signs of the zodiac' (Plate IX)

I will conclude this chapter with something quite simple, just a form of sortilege, which is very popular.[13] It has the merit of being accompanied in the manuscripts by an attractive, and often varied, illustration, which provides the necessary key. And the predictions have a quite traditional flavour.

Many Thai people, while innocent of astrology, have heard of the signs of the zodiac, though knowing nothing of them except that they are twelve in number and supposedly powerful *devas* who could influence their destiny. Being twelve they lend themselves to a means of prognostication in line with the twelve-year cycle and perhaps just as effective as the time-honoured planetary seven. Ignorant of constellations, use is made of a dozen respected symbols to distinguish the 'zodiac' signs.

Three calculations are needed, one for the day, one for the month and one for the year of birth. *Stūpa* is the initial sign, representing either Sunday, the fifth month (from which new year begins), or the Year of the Rat. For a boy one counts from *Stūpa* via Silver Umbrella, for a girl from *Stūpa* via *Nāga*. If two predictions are good, foretell for the good, if two are bad, foretell for the bad, if all three are good, the outlook is indeed good... Here once more, to the curious, the odds seem inviting.

Stūpa or Gold Umbrella. Fortunate, just and with the knowledge of a sage. Will like studying the various 'sciences'. Will be respected everywhere, as a pillar of stability and like a *stūpa* in a monastery. No enemy can harm. Will be moderate in attention to women, agreeable to nobles, Brahmans and the aged. Will receive rich presents and rewards and will live long. But if taken ill it is due to the throne spirit and the *Devacara* (Walking Devatā) for which see page 34.

Silver Umbrella. Will have rank, be helpful and respected everywhere. Enemies will be unable to harm. Will desire all kinds of knowledge, and probably become a sage. Trustworthy and good-natured. Will believe able to protect self from all dangers, perhaps too confidently, for the *devatā* may cause illness.

Decapitated person. Lawsuits will come, will lose money and valued possessions. Will be poor, without support, and will suffer continually.

Palace. Will have sufficient rank, and will be a support to all; but with little personal gain. Will like women and Brahmans. Someone will help to protect from danger, so enemies will be unable to harm. If taken ill it will be the house spirit.

Golden Shrine. Will have rank, and the nobles will befriend. Agreeable to Brahmans. Will be lucky in establishing position, and will help many. Enemies cannot harm, and high praise will be won; but personal gain will be small. Eventually will reach the top. If taken ill it will be caused by the throne spirit, and one of the city guardian spirits (So'a Mo'aṅ).

Rāhu (better known as a planet). Likely to be an angry and proud type, using rank to oppress. Not very dependable. If hates, will hate deeply; if loves, will love dearly. As an official will probably reach a high rank. Illness may be caused by the house spirit.

Devacara (Walking Devatā). Will not be a stable character, and not likely to stay in one place and build a house. Will have wife and children but will not be tied down by them. Likely to be a ne'er-do-well, getting a living from trading and helping the lords. A person of two faces: when stupid, very stupid; when smart, very smart. Never a middle way and will never settle down. If ill it will be caused by the *Devacara*.

Prisoner wearing cangue collar. Will enjoy fortune and prosperity at first, but trouble will come. Relatives will plan evil. Children, wife and servants cannot be trusted. Likely to have trouble and lawsuits continually. Will be firm, not giving way to anyone. Will gain moderate wealth at times, but when short cannot help anyone. If ill it is the *devatā* that punish.

Sorcerer. The lords will give property and position according to worth.

Sorceress. Will be intelligent, inconstant, and lazy at work. Will prefer to be a mistress of concubines. If a man, likely to have many wives. Yet the nobles and Brahmans will consider a good person, for will never be short of money. If ill it will be caused by the spirits in general.

Nāgarāja. An angry, sharp-tongued person, not afraid of anyone. Lazy and gluttonous. Two faces: good and bad. Miserly. Without shame. Resentful. Would like to have many wives. If ill it will be due to the spirit of the place.

NOTES TO CHAPTER II

1. It is possible that in the ancient East a remembered lucky or unlucky historical occurrence was used to reinforce astrological prediction. The Thai, as we shall see, frequently associate a prediction, even in this system of Chinese origin, with an episode drawn from the Buddhist Jātakas or their version (*Rāmakien*) of the Hindu epic *Rāmāyaṇa*.
2. 'Un Manuscrit Khmèr d'astrologie conservée au Musée Guimet', trans. by Sunseng Sunkimneng, *Arts Asiatiques*, Oct. 1977. Only pp. 1–24.correspond to the Thai treatise we are about to consider. Details are often different, though the Khmer MS. is probably derived from a Thai source.
3. *B* I, pp. 1–36. There are of course variant versions.
4. See Hastings' *Encyclopaedia of Religion and Ethics*, Vol. 3 art. Calendar (Chinese), p. 383, and J. Needham, *Science and Civilization in China*, II, 1956, pp. 357 f. and Table 12.
5. References to Brahmans often occur in unexpected places, even in basically Chinese systems such as this, evidence of the great respect formerly accorded to Brahmans in Buddhist Siam.
6. Slavery in Siam was abolished finally by about the year A. D. 1900.
7. The Chinese 'hare in the moon' corresponds to our 'man in the moon'. And a Hindu name for the moon is Śasī, 'marked like a hare'.
8. The high official virtually replaced the noble of earlier times.
9. *B* III, pp. 1–49. Of the Cambodian manuscript referred to above, pp. 25–28, and the illustrations, are usually comparable to our Thai source, but months are differently arranged, and days omitted. The Satow MSi. from which we take the relevant illustrations, lacks the appropriate text,
10. *B* II, pp. 1–49.
11. The terms used are Pāli, evidently derived from those used in some old Tha. (originally Indian) astrological treatises. Cf. Zoro, op.cit., pp. 2, 39.
12. *B* II, p. 51.
13. *B* I, pp. 43 ff.

CHAPTER III

THE MORE IMMEDIATE

The 'Zodiac' again

Whatever the fortune-teller's original promise, there is an ever-recurring desire to know the more immediate outlook. The more sophisticated person in possession of a birth horoscope can readily get an astrologer to cast an annual or 'progressed' horoscope for the coming year. But popular methods are always available. Perhaps the most ready to hand is the 'signs of the zodiac' once more, but this time calculated on the basis of one sign to each year of age, and circulating from *stūpa* in the same manner as previously (Plate IX). Now the portents are as follows, and they do not err on the side of vagueness.[1]

Stūpa: Will obtain all kinds of wealth, as well as a wife, cattle and poultry. If there is a lawsuit, will certainly win it.

Gold or Silver Umbrella: Wealth as desired.

Decapitated: Penalties of all sorts, and blood will flow.

Palace or Golden Shrine. Will gain property of all kinds, house and food as desired, also animals. Much better off than the neighbours.

Rāhu or Nāgarāja: Will be ill with headache and eye trouble; indeed with pains everywhere. Beware of attack; blood will flow.

Devacara: Will gain wealth continually.

Sorcerer: Will obtain wealth and rank, with the help of a noble.

Sorceress: A woman of rank will give you all the wealth you desire, and you will obtain promotion.

The Three-staged Parasol

We pass now to a somewhat more developed variaton, known in the treatises by the above title.[2] It derives part of its power from supposed association with celebrated 'historical' events known to all.[3] And it requires a diagrammatic plan as set out in Fig. 3.

THE MORE IMMEDIATE

	N.E.	Rāma E.	S.E.	
Pipek	8 6 1	6 1 2	1 2 3	Bimbisāra
Hanumān N.	5 8 4	0	4 3 2	S. Lak
Sadāyu	8 5 7	5 7 4	7 4 3	Tosakanth
	N.W.	W. Sīdā	S.W.	

Fig. 3

To know his immediate prospects a man takes his age, less one year,[4] and circulates from Rāma via Bimbisāra. A woman takes her age, less one year, and circulates from Sīdā via Sadāyu. Each counts one square for each year until the age is reached. However the year is considered as divided into three four-month periods: months 5, 6, 7, 8 = the inner number of square; months 9, 10, 11, 12 = middle number of square; months 1, 2, 3, 4 = outer numbers. This affords a greater degree of refinement, thus:

1 Inside N.E. Where the giant Pipek (Vibhīshana), brother of Tosakanth (Rāvana), stands: Family will be afflicted, quarrelling together, and there will be separation from children, wife and servants. There will be much trouble, will leave home and suffer punishment and anguish.

6 Middle N.E. Pipek meets Rāma. This is very lucky, top of the world. Desires will be met. Travel for trade will be profitable. If an official, will be promoted.

8 Outer N.E. Pipek goes to rule Langkā. This is a good omen. Desires will be met, wealth and rank attained. Later there will be illness from which one will groan with pain. Set up a statue to Pipek. Make offerings of tasty foods and garlands to him and to the lord of the north-east. The illness will disappear.

2 Inside E. Rāma rules, when he gains Sīdā. Excellent portents. The Brahmans will make you presents and you will have a young and beautiful woman who will cherish you. All will be as you wish: including clothes and ornaments. If you travel you will gain abundant profit. And being a successful man don't forget to make offerings.

1 Middle E. Rāma when away from Sīdā, so sorrows will come. You will be separated from children, wife, and relatives, and will lose servants and goods. Very weighty losses. With such bad portents, don't travel. You will be cheated in business, and above all, there is danger of losing your beloved wife.

6 Outer E. When Rāma retrieved Sīdā, a very good portent. If you wish to go to war you will be very strong. You will be very happy with children and wife. Even if you lose your wealth you will get it back. If spirits annoy, quickly make an image of Rāma holding a trident, two images of demons, and one of Death. Make offerings to them and to the East, as already prescribed. The evil will disappear, and you will enjoy every happiness.

3 Inner S.E. Bimbisāra, when his son seized the kingdom. This is a most evil omen. Relatives will seize land and servants. Sorrow will result from the attacks of wicked children.

2 Middle S.E. Bimbisāra's kingdom when the king attained the first degree of sanctity. Portents very good; will obtain anything desired, and live in happiness with joyful loving family.

1 Outer S.E. When King Bimbisāra died he went to heaven; the portent is both good and bad. First there will be affliction, afterwards perfection and great happiness will be attained. Fever will burn like fire and robber spirits molest. Quickly prepare offerings. Make an image of the lord, holding a trident; also of three demons and a separate one of Death. Then make offerings to the southeast. The illness and molestation will vanish, and you will be well. Appetite and working ability good.

4 Inner S. Lak (Lakshman) when he became a monk. Very good portent. Will obtain anything you desire; but beware a wanton attractive widow who will sigh with love for you. Don't become intimate, she will certainly deceive you.

3. Middle S. Lak when he was pierced by the Mohasak spear (of Kumbhakarn). A severe portent. Look to hands and feet. You'll need weapons, and spikes on the path. Much trouble and blood will flow. Beware of a bad man.

2 Outer S. Lak when he was freed from this spear. Very good. Will be a powerful person who will conquer enemies. If fever strikes, quickly prepare offerings, as detailed above.

7 Inner S.W. Rāvana when he stole Sīdā. A grand portent. First will be happy, but later will rue the day. There will be a serious accident: beware of robbers and fire, and of a woman associate who will do harm.

4 Middle S.W. Rāvana, when he made a deva build Langkā. A moderately good portent. Till the fields and get good harvests; or if an official will gain desires and be very happy.

3 Outer S.W. Rāvana, who spent the wealth of Langkā. Very bad portent. Don't travel afar, for you will run into disease and danger; you'll be ruined. If you get fever it will be fatal. Calamity and failure threaten. Immediately offer sacrifices to avert the evil. Make an image of the demon, holding in the hand a *tapong* charm. make seven images of other demons and one of Death. Make offerings to the south-west. The suffering will disappear. You will gain what you desire and triumph over your enemies.

5 Inner W. Sīdā when she became the wife of Rāma. Excellent portent. You will gain all desires. If you become a courtier you will attain high rank and happiness. If a woman you will get a husband of good position. A man will get a beautiful wife —through the help of an old Brahman.

7 Middle W. Sīdā when separated from Rāma, a very bad portent. Much sadness and anguish. A wicked person will deceive by wile. If a woman, will leave husband; if a man, will be long separated from wife.

4 Outer W. Beautiful Sīdā when she came from Langkā. Very good portent. You will get your desires and rejoice with relatives long separated. Make a beautiful image (of Sīdā), also four of demons and one of Death. Then make offerings to the west. You will recover and be happy.

8 Inner N.W. Powerful Sadāyu, killed by Sīdā's ring (thrown by Rāvana). A very bad presage. Fear for self, fear for pledged objects and fear a lawsuit. A subordinate may harm you by substituting an object.

5 Middle N.W. Sadāyu when raised by Viṣṇu. Very favourable.

A high lord will help you, and whatever you undertake will prosper. You'll have abundance of cattle, land and servants.

7 Outer N.W. When Rāvana fought with Sadāyu. A very bad portent. Fear for children. Something shameful will occur. There will be a lawsuit and tumult. You will quarrel with a man who comes from afar, and there will be trouble over a wicked girl. If the house spirits make you ill, make an image of a *yakṣa*, holding a trident, eight figures of demons and an image of Death. Make them suitable offerings; and sacrifice also to the north-west. All illness and trouble will disappear, and you will attain permanent stability.

4 Inner N. Hanumān, when he exerted his strength. Good portent. The lords will give any rewards that you desire.

8 Middle N. This was when Hanumān was tied by Indrajit's serpent Nakabat. A very bad portent. Don't travel—you will meet shame. Fear a crowd of enemies, also fear snakes. There will be alarms, warnings of trouble; but later you will triumph over your enemies.

5 Outer N. Splendid Hanumān, when he came from Langkā. The portent is one of supreme victory. While away from home you will receive property and presents, servants and rank. If you are made ill by frightening dreams, make an image of a forest monkey, also images of six demons and a separate one of Death. Also sacrifice to the north. Illness will disappear, you can eat, sleep and be happy.

The most important point to note in the above is the attachment of the cardinal and sub-cardinal points to events in the much venerated *Rāmakien*, certainly a good reason for popular preference for such divination, as compared to astrology. The fact that Rāvana is regarded as somewhat of a hero, makes any temporary success of his rather a good omen. We also note, whatever the portent, a deep-seated recognition of the need to propitiate gods, demons and local spirits.

Planets Ruling Age.[5]

We come now to a system that is widely considered to be of great importance. It is especially, though not exclusively, used to determine the outlook at one's present age, and the likelihood of success of a particular undertaking. It is closely related to astrology and its Hindu origin is beyond doubt. Indeed Dubois describes what is unmistakably the same system as being in vogue in India in the early nineteenth century.[6] It is also referred to by Sir George Scott as being the most popular form of 'horoscope' calculated in Burma, because readily understood by the people.[7] But it is Sangermano who provided the best account of its use there.[8] All the above authors stress that in this system it is the influence of the four planets of the cardinal points, Moon, Mercury, Jupiter and Venus, that is considered favourable, that of the sub-cardinal points, Sun, Mars, Saturn and Rāhu being the reverse. This is obviously understood to be the case in the Thai system. The planet Rāhu not having a day, anyone born after mid-day on Wednesday is considered to be associated with this shadowy planet.

It is supposed that these eight planetary deities rule over our lives for unequal periods, starting from the day of birth. At the end of each period the next takes over, the order being that of the position of the planets, starting with the Sun at the north-east. Thus Sun rules for 6 years, Moon for 15, Mars for 8, Mercury for 17, Saturn for 10, Jupiter for 19, Rāhu for 12 and Venus for 21 years, total 108, an astrologically significant number. But each planet rules alone for only a small initial part of the period, after which the rule is shared with each of the other planetary deities in turn for a greater or lesser

Rāhu N.W. 12 yrs. Wednesday p.m.	Venus N. 21 yrs. Friday	Sun N.E. 6 yrs. Sunday
Jupiter W. 19 yrs. Thursday		Moon E. 15 yrs. Monday
Saturn S.W. 10 yrs. Saturday	Mercury S. 17 yrs. Wednesday a.m.	Mars S.E. 8 yrs. Tuesday

Fig. 4.

portion of the remaining period. The sharing planet, acting in some sense as minister, has the power to modify the rule, more or less favourably according to his character, during the period when he shares control.

Sun rules for 6 years

Sun alone (4 months). Not very good.
Sun with Moon (10m), will have worries; propitiate both deities for 15 days, and will then be fortunate.
Sun with Mars (5m 10 days), not very good. Propitiate both to avert evil.
Sun with Mercury (11m 10d), good. Propitiate both and will gain many kinds of good fortune.
Sun with Saturn (6m 20d). Outlook bad; propitiate both to avert evil.
Sun with Jupiter (1yr 20d). Will obtain wealth.
Sun with Rāhu (8m). Will lose money. Propitiate to avert evil.
Sun with Venus (1yr 2m). Will gain wealth, elephants and horses, slaves male and female. If you go north or south will be fortunate.

Moon rules for 15 years

Moon alone (2yrs 1m), will gain wealth, coming from N. or S.
Moon with Mars (1yr 1m 10d). Not good, will lose money. Propitiate.
Moon with Mercury (2yrs 4m 10d). Will gain wealth, brought by friends from N. and S. Make offerings to both planets and all will be well.
Moon with Saturn (1yr 4m 20d). Not good; fear enemies; propitiate to avert evil.
Moon with Jupiter (2yrs 7m 20d). Husband and wife liable to quarrel; beware a fair woman living E. or W. Later will be fortunate.
Moon with Rāhu (1yr 8m). Fear trouble over a woman.
Moon with Venus (2yrs 11m). Will gain wealth (jewels, gold and silver).
Moon with Sun (10m). Fear darkish man from N.E. or S.W. Propitiate to avert evil.

THE MORE IMMEDIATE

Mars rules for 8 years

Mars alone (7m 3d 20mins). Not good, indeed very dangerous.

Mars with Mercury (1yr 3m 3d 20mins). Will gain wealth from friends coming from N., S. and E.

Mars with Saturn (8m 26d 40mins). Beware of being concerned in disputes, the danger coming from S.W. and N. Propitiate to avert evil.

Mars with Jupiter (1yr 4m 26d 40mins). Will gain wealth (silver and gold), but must beware of a fair woman and a dark man living to the E., S.E. or W. They will slander.

Mars with Rāhu (10m 20d). Fear fire will burn house. Propitiate, then will enjoy good fortune.

Mars with Venus (1yr 6m 20d). Will gain wealth (gold and silver) from N. and S.E. If you propitiate both deities will become truly wealthy.

Mars with Sun (5m 10d). Fear loss of wife and children and house burnt. Enemies are to the N.E. and S.E. Propitiate, to avert evil.

Mars and Moon (1yr 1m 10d). Will gain wealth from a fair woman who lives to the E. or S. If slaves run away they will be returned.

Mercury rules for 17 years

Mercury alone (2yrs 8m 3d 20mins). If you are of good family and well-behaved you will be successful, have much wealth and many attendants.

Mercury with Saturn (1yr 6m 26d 40mins). Beware that from a dispute over a dark woman you will lose valued possessions; and also fear that two dark men living to the S.W. or N. will harm you. Propitiate.

Mercury with Jupiter (2yrs 11m 26d 40mins). If you travel you will have trouble, but if you stay at home you will have a desirable wife and children.

Mercury with Rāhu (1yr 10m 20d). Fear a paunchy dark person who will do harm, and fire will burn house. Enemies are to the N.W. and S.E. Propitiate both deities to avert evil.

Mercury with Venus (3yrs 3m 20d). You will gain silver and gold, clothing and slaves, both male and female, with the aid of a fair and a dark woman, or friends. This wealth will come from the N. and S.E.

Mercury with Sun (11m 10d). Disputes likely; move to the E.; propitiate.

Mercury with Moon (2yrs 4m 10d). Will gain silver, gold, children, wives, slaves of both sexes, because of friends. Also wealth from E. & S.

Mercury with Mars (1yr 3d 20mins). There will be disputes, and fire will burn the house. Dark enemies will come from N.E. and S.E. Beware of them, and propitiate both planets to avert the evil.

Saturn rules for 10 years

Saturn alone (11m 3d 20mins). Will have trouble over parents, lose wealth and be ill. Enemies will meditate harm. Relatives will die and fire burn the house. Propitiate, to avert the evil.

Saturn and Jupiter (1yr 9m 3d 20mins). If you go W. you will be in danger; but elsewhere, away from home, a great teacher will reward. Propitiate, then all well.

Saturn with Rāhu (1yr 1m 10d). Fear something that will happen in ten days. Don't eat flesh or fowl. Propitiate the two planets and later you will gain wealth.

Saturn with Venus (1yr 11m 10d). Fear two enemies living in N. and S.W. who will bring trouble. Propitiate to avert evil.

Saturn with Sun (6m 20d). You will spend money on account of wife and children. Don't go S.W. or N.E. as danger lurks there. Propitiate to avert the evil.

Saturn with Moon (1yr 4m 20d). You will gain wealth, wives and children. But you must propitiate both deities.

Saturn with Mars (8m 26d 40mins). Danger of losing money, wives and children, also friends. A dark enemy is to the S.E. or N.W. planning evil.

Saturn with Mercury (1yr 6m 26d 40mins). Don't eat flesh or fowl if you would avoid stomach trouble. Your enemy is a dark woman with threatening wide-opened eyes, who lives to the N.W. If you go to the jungle an enemy will harm you. Propitiate, and later gain wealth.

Jupiter rules for 19 years

Jupiter rules alone (3yrs 4m 3d 20mins). You will be great and wealthy. You will obtain animals, children, wives, slaves of both sexes—and a good reputation.

Jupiter with Rāhu (2yrs 1m 10d). You will have stomach trouble, and there will be evil omens. A beloved will become your enemy. Beware a paunchy man with curly hair living to N.W., W., or S.E.

Jupiter with Venus (3yrs 8m 10d). You will gain wealth from a fair woman who loves you. She will come from the N. Any work will succeed.

Jupiter with Sun (1yr 1m 20d). Danger of suffering from ear and eye trouble, this illness being caused by the house spirits. Propitiate the two planets, and later you will gain wealth from friends and persons of rank, coming from the N.E. or N.

Jupiter with Moon (2yrs 7m 20d). You will lose wealth and be ruined by an enemy. Fear a fair woman living to E. and S. Later you will regain wealth.

Jupiter with Mars (1yr 4m 26d 40mins). Fear a noble who will throw you into chains or bring a case against you. Take great care.

Jupiter with Mercury (2yrs 10m 26d 40mins). You will gain silver and gold, cattle and poultry; also a good reputation. If in a lawsuit you will have a good advocate. The wealth will come from the S. Make offerings to both planets, and you will get even more.

Jupiter with Saturn (1yr 9m 3d 20mins). Fear the loss of silver and gold because of a powerful man; or the high officials will punish you. A dark man may slander. If you are ill go and live to the N.W. And propitiate to avert the evil.

Rāhu rules for 12 years

Rāhu rules alone (1yr 4m). You will have trouble and illness. Blood will flow. Fear being cast into chains. You will lose silver and gold, and parents will die. If ill, move to the S.W. Propitiate Rāhu to avert the evil.

Rāhu with Venus (2yrs 4m). You will gain wealth, coming from N. and S.E.

Rāhu with Sun (8m). A great man will make you wealthy. Later you will suffer from headache and eye trouble. You will spend money for a beloved. If ill move S.W. or W. But fear a dark enemy living to the S.W. Propitiate both planets and become rich.

Rāhu with Moon (1yr 8m). The lords will be angry with you or your slaves will flee. If a lawsuit occurs you will lose. Fear a fair man and woman living to N.E. Propitiate the planets and later become rich.

Rāhu with Mars (10m 20d). Fear slaves will slander. You will lose silver and gold, and blood will flow. If ill, move to the N. Propitiate both planets, to avert evil.

Rāhu with Mercury (1yr 10m 20d). You will gain silver and gold, but later an enemy will calumniate and you will lose wealth. If ill move to the N. Propitiate, to avert evil.

Rāhu with Saturn (1yr 1m 10d). Fear trouble in ten days. Don't eat flesh or fowl. Don't climb trees or big hills. Fear a dark enemy living to N.E. or S.W. Later you will gain wealth through friends, this wealth coming from the N.W.

Rāhu with Jupiter (2yrs 1m 10d). You will have stomach trouble and bad omens. A beloved will become your enemy. A corpulent man with curly hair living to the N.W. or S.E. is to be feared. Propitiate.

Venus rules for 21 years

Venus alone (4yrs 1m). You will gain wealth, clothes, gold and silver, also happiness. The wealth will come from the N. and S.E.

Venus with Sun (1yr 2m). Will have various illnesses and fear of suffering on account of friends. Or wife will do wrong and fire will burn the house. Be careful of what you say for fear of starting a lawsuit.

Venus with Moon (2yrs 11m). An old man living to the east will give gold and silver.

Venus with Mars (1yr 6m 20d). You will get wealth, goods, wives and children. If you do government work you will gain a good reputation and attain rank. If you go to war you will win. If a woman you will get an agreeable husband.

Venus with Mercury (3yrs 3m 20d). You will gain wealth, coming

from the E., in which direction you should move if you are ill. Propitiate both planets and gain much wealth.
Venus with Saturn (1yr 11m 10d). Will leave wife and children, lose money, and slaves will run away. If ill move to the N.W. Propitiate to avert the evil.
Venus with Jupiter (3yrs 8m 10d) Much wealth and the lords will give high rank and position.
Venus with Rāhu (2yrs 4m). Fear of losing wealth to a darkish enemy, with threatening staring eyes. He lives to the N.W. and S.E. You will be very ill; children, wives and relations will die. If ill, move to the S.W. Propitiate, to avert the evil.

While, as I have said, this system of prognostication is most frequently appealed to in order to determine the likelihood of success in a particular undertaking in the near future, I am given to understand that at the present day many Thais are still assiduous in making the prescribed offerings to the planetary deities that rule over their time of life. The prescribed offerings, as laid down in the treatises,[9] may be summarized as follows: Offerings of flowers, tapers, areca and betel should be made to both the ruling and the associate *devas*, in amounts and over a number of days proportionate to the years of rule of each *deva*. A short appeal to the deity concerned should then be recited three times. A wax candle of one *bāt* weight should be lit for the ruling planet, and one of $\frac{1}{2}$ *bāt* for the associate. At noon one must sit in meditation facing the east, and must then pronounce another appeal to the particular *deva*. At the same time Buddhism is associated with the practice by the setting up of a specific Buddha image for each of the planets concerned. Thus for the Sun, a meditating Buddha, for Moon a Buddha calming the ocean, for Saturn a Buddha seated on the *nāga*, and so on.[10]

Portentous Pimples

Another form of divination which lends itself, though again not exclusively, to discovering the immediate outlook is provided by the consideration of pimples. By their very nature many types of pimples can appear suddenly, at any age, thereby suggesting that they convey a revelation as to the near future. I should not like to be dogmatic as to the proximate direction from which this form of divination reached the Thai, but I think that an ultimately Indian origin is likely. It is certainly attested for the Buddhist kingdom over which ruled King Milinda. In answer to a question from the king, the monk Nāgasena replied 'According to the places on which the pimples have arisen, the fortune-tellers, making their observations, give decision, saying "Such and such will be the result".'[11] Again Varāhamihira, the famous sixth century A.D. Indian astronomer cum astrologer (though the chapter is suspected of being a later interpolation), gives a list of the omens to be derived from what Kern translates as the 'marks of boils', but I think should more properly be understood as pimples.[12] Except on one point to which I shall refer later, his list parallels, rather than coincides with, the Thai conceptions.

In the Thai treatises[13] a characteristic emphasis is placed on the advice that one should on no account place too much reliance on the deductions to made from pimples, but should weigh them together with any other portents that may be available. Thus if the findings from pimples and palmistry are bad, but other portents are good, the outlook should be regarded as mixed.

Facial pimples, unlike those on the body, are more often unfortunate than the reverse, especially for men. Good ones are black or vermilion, not so are red, white and yellow ones. If slight, the ill effect will be mild. Those in groups of seven or five are especially favourable: if on the left they denote wealth, if on the right, promotion. A pimple on the left eyebrow indicates property, on the right longevity. A black spot in the hair suggests prosperity, still more so if it is prominent. If a group of seven are arranged on the forehead in the W-shape of the constellation Cassiopeia, this is most lucky. A pimple on the ear lobe signifies intelligence, long life if inside the ear. Between the eyebrows indicates prosperity, if on the tip of the ear the prosperity will continue. A pimple on the eyeball means that person will be grateful to parents. If it is situated above the middle of the upper lip it is lucky, especially if black or red; otherwise only moderately so.

The following facial pimples are unfavourable: at the start of the lower jaw, below the hair line, unless very small. They mean trouble. A pimple in the middle of the forehead means one is likely to lose father or mother. If it is in the corner of an eye, just where the tears emerge, one will have continuing sorrow. If it is over the cheek bone it is not at all good: that unlucky person, if he has rank, will be demoted; if he has any wealth, he will lose it. If it is just at the middle of the nostrils he will be poor. If at the edge, not good, and this is also the case if the pimple is on the ear lobe or near the opening. If it is at the tip of the nose he is likely to have trouble with his feet! And if on the sides of the nose, property will be lost. A pimple over the mouth means that person will be likely to suffer for his remarks; while one near the mouth indicates extravagance. A pimple at the corner of the eye, or a little away, portends an unfortunate marriage. Pimples under the chin are lucky. If black ones appear all over the face, this is bad in the young, but good in older people.

As already stated, pimples on the body are more likely to be lucky especially in a hidden place. They often come in pairs. Black pimples, under the forearm and going down to the hand, are not good, one is likely to be ill. But if near the wrist, that is good and money will come. If right in the elbow bend—much money. But a pimple *on* the elbow is not good. If one is situated on the back of the shoulder one will become a good craftsman. If under the armpits one will become wealthy and have consequent peace of mind. A pimple near the front depression of the collar-bone is ill-omened, and if on the middle of the front of the collar-bone thefts are to be expected.

A pimple on the middle of the shoulder or in front of it, signifies trouble, but on the back of it means money coming. A pimple on the palm or on the back of the hand portends prosperity. One on the front of the knee indicates the possession of many slaves. At the top of the back of the leg signifies prosperity, and so does one on or under the knee. Pimples on the front of the leg herald fame, and if on the sole of the foot one will be a lord. A pimple near the toes means many slaves, and on the breast many children. If under the breast one will be wealthy; if between the breasts will live long and be happy A pimple in the navel signifies prosperity and good children, on both sides of the navel prosperity and happiness. If on the throat, above the Adam's apple, one will have constant helpers, but not so good if it is below the apple, while one behind the throat indicates power. A pimple over the middle of the spine portends long life. One in the middle of the waist means must go and live at a distance, while one on the hips suggests wealth and rank.

I have reserved to the last the one point on which Varāhamihira and the Thai treatises exhibit close agreement. According to the latter a pimple on the tip of the *liṅga* portends that the owner will be blessed with good children. For Varāhamihira, a similar appearance, in the words of Kern's translation, 'on the *membrum virile*, brings a damsel and fine children'. Diffusion or independent origin?

NOTES TO CHAPTER III

1 *B* I, pp. 48 ff.
2 *B* II, pp. 53 ff.
3 Bimbisāra was king of Magadha, killed by his son Ajātasatru; the other personages are characters in the *Rāmakien*.
4 One year is deducted because the Thai commonly count themselves a year old on the day of birth.
5 *B* I, pp. 62 ff.
6 Dubois, op.cit., p. 379.
7 Scott, op. cit., p. 9.
8 Sangermano, *The Burmese Empire a hundred years ago*, London, 1893, p. 147.
9 *B* I, pp. 77 ff.
10 In his book *Thai Buddhism*, Bangkok, 1939, pp. 200 f., Kenneth E. Wells mentions that in the ceremony of 'Releasing of Bad Luck' on the king's birthday, the Brahmanic texts have since 1878 been replaced by Buddhist *gathas*, repeated in accordance with the 'auspicious number' of the planet. This number evidently coincides with what we have seen are the planet's years of rule. However, in his list, the ninth planet Ketu is accorded the number 9, although this planet does not appear to have any period of rule.
11 *Questions of King Milinda, Sacred Books of the East*, XXXVI, pp. 158 f.
12 *The Bṛhat-Samhitā of Varāhamihira*, Chapter LII, trans H. Kern, *Verspreide Geschriften*, Vol. I. (from *Journ. Royal Asiatic Soc.* 1870–75).
13 *B* III, pp. 82 ff.

CHAPTER IV
PALMISTRY

The study of pimple predictions that we have just considered is classed as a branch of physiognomy, and allied to this is palmistry (or chiromancy), although a generally accepted characteristic is that the basic indications of the hand do not change throughout life. Chinese and Western (or Indian) palmistry are very different, and what we find in the traditional Thai treatises is Chinese. How long this Chinese palmistry has been popular in Siam it is impossible to say. Manuscripts on the subject are lacking in the Bangkok National Library, and it seems to me likely that the art was long practised by Chinese fortune-tellers before books from China were translated into Thai and printed about the middle of last century. In the Thai historical novel *Khun Chang Khun Phan* the Lawas of the north are mentioned as noted for their knowledge of palmistry.[1] Perhaps they obtained it from their Shan contacts.

At the present time one has only to notice the placards of the street practitioners in Bangkok to realize that Western methods are competing with the Chinese form in the metropolis. But in general I think the Chinese form still maintains the traditional priority, and booklets advocating its use by employers for testing job-applicants are widely sold. Palmistry is generally supposed to have been derived from astrology, and the great difference between the Chinese and Western methods is that the former places more reliance on the 'mounts' than on the lines. Needham has remarked that he was unable to ascertain how far Chinese palmistry was an indigenous growth.[2] Apart from an article by Arlington,[3] little has been published in western languages on the Chinese art, which adds to the interest of examining here the Thai borrowing. In Burma Sangermano refers to the practice of palmistry, but what little detail he gives suggests the Indian form.[4]

PALMISTRY

The Palms in general

The traditional Thai-adopted treatise[5] which I utilize gives us the following information: It starts with the important notification that flesh and bone must be well adapted *inter se*. It is not good if bones stick out or flesh does not adhere closely to the bones. This indicates poverty, just as well rounded flesh indicates prosperity. Too much bone and too little flesh means one cannot depend on rlatives. Good hand characteristics are: palm soft, like cotton, skin as delicate as precious stuff, hand lines like silken threads. The hand should be reddish and never cold. The back of the hand should be arched like the back of a tortoise. The centre of the palm should be deep, like an egg-shell. Bones and wrist should be smooth, not swollen, skin not too tight and flesh thick. Palms like this indicate prosperity and wealth. Bad signs are: palms that are hard and rough to the touch, dry and dark with swollen sinews and prominent bones, skinny hands in fact. Trouble and a short life may be expected.

For a young person to have large palms but small fingers suggests he is never likely to be rich. Palms the colour of pig's liver mean the likelihood of going to war, or of otherwise having to leave home. Thin palms in a thin person do not matter but are a bad sign in a fat person, while fat palms are of good augury in both fat and thin people. If palms are good but lines bad, one will be poor when young; if the reverse one will be comfortably off when old. A dark red pimple on the palm signifies both wealth and good luck. Unusual lines on the palm foretell rank and position. With prominent sinews and bones one may be materially well-off but will be sad at heart. With finger joints swollen and fingers separated that person is likely to be an idler. With palms yellow and cold one is liable to start in sleep; but if warm and blood-red, from youth to age one will never know illness. If the left palm is lined and the right palm is not, one will have few relations.

The palms should change with the seasons as follows: In the hot season, they must sweat; in the rainy season be clean and damp, in the cold season dry. If in the hot season palms become dry, and in the cold season sweaty, that person will meet trouble. Sinews should not project but lie close, if wealth is to be gained. The palm of the hand being paler than the back of it, portends wealth; the opposite poverty.

Lines are of very secondary importance to the mounts, to be dealt with below. But good lines, narrow and deep, not joining or broken, do indicate intelligence. Those that have definite shapes of objects, seals, letters or animals are good; the opposite if without shape or unclear. If the lines go straight up into the fingers, that person will complete any work as he may wish; if the lines are entwined like silk threads he will be intelligent. If the lines are as rough as a file that person and his family will be poor; but if they are like rice husks scattered all over the palm he will be happy through life. If they are like small crosses, descending from mounts, 5, 6 and 7 (Fig. 5), that person will have much happiness. If there are superimposed chevrons in mount 2, he will have prosperity and many descendants; if three crosses disposed in a triangle, much intelligence and great success. If there are crosses below two fingers, descending downwards, he will ask help from someone who will bring him into the family. A single chevron indicates great intelligence. If the lines are like fish scales he will lean on a relative who will be very affectionate. A fish's tail on the thumb indicates wealth and so does chessboard marking.

If a cross fills the palm one will be born wealthy and gain power too. A square like a seal, clearly formed, in the middle of the palm, indicates wealth from youth. Three squares in decreasing pyramidal series means one will become a noble. Irregular cross-hatching on the palm, stretching from thumb down to mount 3, means one will suffer from morbid thoughts. A row of three concentric circles indicates riches. A square or a triangle, a seal figure, if in the middle of the hand, means that person will be trustworthy, will never suffer punishment or be in danger, and will be brave, with no fear of malignant spirits or of anything else. If such a person associates with the great he will attain power. If the triangle or seal figure is above the wrist to mount 2, that person will be addicted to sensual pleasures. If it is below the little finger, that is not good. But situated in the centre of the hand long life is indicated. Its extending into the middle finger is lucky, still more so if it extends into all the fingers. Concentric circles mean that one will have the support of a good woman.

A line having the form of a seal or letter is always good; if it resembles a belt buckle that means prosperity to the person and all his family—provided it is not broken or distorted. If lines form a narrow rectangle, that is called the coffin figure. It is bad and very important. It can come at any time between the base of the thumb and mount 3. Only if imperfect or cut by other lines is it not important. But it is very ill-omened if it is complete or blackish, or white. Any year it appears, the effect will follow during that year. If one such figure appears, you'll have trouble over anything you do. If two, you'll lose a relative or dear friend. If three, various kinds of sorrows. If four, you'll die. If a coffin figure, plus that of a shell, appears, you'll commit suicide.

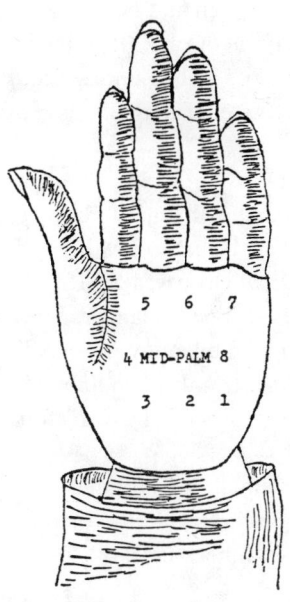

Fig. 5

The mounts or divisions of the palm[6]

These relate to:

1. Father, mother, and older relatives.
2. Wealth and inheritance.
3. Relatives and cultivated lands.
4. Wife, lesser and greater.
5. Obtainable wealth.
6. Rank and position.
7. Male and female children.
8. Slaves and servants.

Mid-palm concerns the character of the individual.

1. If small or mutilated, will be an orphan. If flesh there prominent will have good children and be prosperous. If a line from here to 6, parents will attain high rank. If a line aslant to 5, parents will have trouble. If a line to 7 will be unmarried. If a line to 3 will have to go and work elsewhere. If many lines cross 1, inherited wealth cannot be kept.

2. If small or mutilated, will inherit nothing from parents. If fleshy will inherit from father. If line to 6 will be very lucky and wealthy. If line to 5, not good; will lose wealth. If to 7 will lose children; and wife and her relatives will be in danger. Indeed must marry two or three times. If 2 is crossed by many silk-like lines it means accession of wealth from a noble. If unbroken lines come up to 2 from wrist, this means will rise to prosperity by own efforts.

3. If this mount is small or mutilated it indicates that there will be difficulty in bringing up a family, or relatives will quarrel. If a line to 4, one will gain inheritance.

4. If this is small or mutilated, that person will be poorly married. If fleshy will be rich, with residence and cultivated land. If 4 is crossed by many lines, this means that spouse is likely to be anxious or ill.

5. If small or mutilated, will lose property. But if prominent and of blood-red colour this indicates much property. If it is the most prominent of all the divisions, it means continually increasing wealth and good luck from childhood. If there is a cross-hatched line not reaching to the finger this means a miserly disposition. If it extends to the palm, or between thumb and index, wealth cannot be kept. If from 5 a dotted black line loops round 1 it means that person will be bitten by a snake.

6. If this is small or mutilated, one cannot get rank and position; but if prominent will be lucky and high ranking. If a black line connects with 2 will die of want.

7. If small or mutilated, will rear children with difficulty and not be likely to succeed. If crossed by lines this is not good. If prominent, raising children will be easy and will have many. A crowsfoot figure on 7 is good.

8. If small or mutilated will have few slaves and servants. If prominent, the opposite.

Some further indications: if mounts 5, 6 and 7 are all prominent this is very lucky. If only 5 is prominent, beneath index and pointing downwards, this signifies rank and fortune; if only a swelling on 7 pointing downwards from little finger, this means all kinds of prosperity. If a figure like this + extends over 7 and 8, one will get property from a woman, but if crossed by other lines will lose it to a woman. If 4 has many lines one will have a very severe-speaking spouse, or will be ill. If 7 has the figure of a crowsfoot, one will win money as a gamester. If a woman has mount 4 prominent, of soft red flesh, or has a series of circles or a seal figure there, she'll be very lucky and have more authority than a man. But if 7 is low or has lines diverging from it, she'll be poor and not able to keep money.

Mid-palm: this is very important since it tells of 'heart', i. e. character. If it is clear one won't have any important business. If a straight unbent line passes across it one will be a faithful person. If the line is deep, one who considers deeply, the opposite if it is shallow. If the line is very wide, one will not be realiable. If there are many lines one is likely to be a thinker, the opposite if lines are few. If the line is entangled so will be one's thought. If lines are touching or close together, one will do things easily, and spoil them easily too. If the lines are dispersed, one is likely to be very lazy. (Nothing, one might comment, shows more clearly the close connection between brain and hand.)

Happy or sad

If your face is dark but your nose is clear and your palms show blood-red, you'll be happy at first but later you'll be sad. If your face is clear but your nose is dark and your palms don't show blood-red, one thing is certain: you'll be sad before you're glad. If an expectant mother has palms of greenish red, the child will be a boy; but if they're darkish white, then a girl is on the way. An easy birth if palms are clear, the contrary if they're faded.

About illness

Examine the patient: if he looks thin but his fingers show blood-red, and the tip of his nose is clean and bright—it's not serious. But if he's dark between the eyebrows and his nose is green, if his ears are dark and his eyes wander—there's no cure. If all ten finger-nails are black, and on his palm is the figure of a coffin, which goes up to mount 3—death will take him that day.

Fingers

The following are the seven good characteristics of fingers: round and well-polished; fat; straight, not bent; pointed tips; well adjusted, showing no light between them; clear and blood-coloured; not bent back.

Then come the seven bad characteristics: crooked; atrophied, flat or too small; contracted; thin or monstrously big; joints bent forwards or backwards; widely separated, with ends like pestle tops; bases swollen like knots. Fingers bending outwards mean that person will probably leave home and owing to trouble will have to get a living elsewhere. Atrophied fingers portend loss of wealth; too small ones cannot make a living and if in government work will be demoted. Fingers too short, the person will be very poor; if contracted and liable to tire, will have to seek food everywhere; if thin or broken, will lose wealth; if monstrously big, will lose property and be dissatisfied; if bent back will be very poor and without support.

Fingers widely separated means that members of the family are not likely to be amicable. If gaps between the fingers, cannot keep money. If very hard, likely to be poor. If bases of fingers swollen and upper parts short and knotty, like the tops of pestles, life will be short. If flesh is separated from nails, wealth will be absent in middle life. If there's a line round the four fingers, leaving aside the little one, it is a bad sign, but one round the little finger is good. It is also a good sign if the base of the middle finger is embraced by a crow's foot figure.

All five fingers of equal length is a sign that that person will be stupid. For the middle finger to be the same length as the palm or longer is very favourable; but if shorter, not so good. Compare the little finger with the thumb: good if of equal length or thumb longer; but if the little finger is longer it means that the father and mother will not enjoy high rank. If the little finger is longer than the index, the owner when young will be rather poor, but will have children when very old on whom can depend for support. If the little and index fingers are of the same length, one will continually gain wealth. Little and middle fingers being the same length donotes wealth and good children. Little and ring fingers being equal indicates skill in craftsmanship and good fortune.

Straightness is important: if the thumb is not straight, the person will get tired and unable to finish work. The same defect in the middle finger means he will only act according to his own conscience; in the ring finger, will have a spouse of similar mind; in the little finger, will have no children, or they will leave home. If index is the largest, will have much wealth and provide amply for family. If it is very short, a man is likely to remain a bachelor or be afraid of his wife.

A tall person with short fingers is headed for trouble. A small person with long fingers will be greedy. If the bases of the fingers are separated, one will be unable to keep money. If separated at the tips, one cannot depend on the support of relatives. If the tips resemble pestles, will be tired and not live long. If the fingers form a series resembling plant shoots, this indicates wealth. If the little and ring fingers start at the same level, it means one will become a high official through knowledge. If thumb and index start at the same level it points to one becoming a high army officer. For fingers to be longer than palm is a good sign, but the opposite means one will be slandered. If the index is long it means one will like to associate with people of rank. If the ring finger is long, will be a constant lover. If any finger gets damaged, one will be punished similarly. If it's the thumb one will lose a senior relative; if its' the middle, will lose mother; if the little finger, a child.

Now to take the fingers separately:

1. The thumb, which has two joints. If a line entwines it at the base this portends that father will die first. If it has on it a line resembling the head of a curved spear, mother will die first.

2. The index finger. This is very important. It should be round, well-polished and straight. It should not be crooked, small, atrophied or mutilated, for if so it is unlucky. If it bends out from the middle finger this indicates much sorrow, exhaustion from going hither and thither looking for a living.

3. Middle finger, also very important. It must be straight. If it is bent back this portends want, and if there is the bottom of a shell mark on it, no work can be finished. A good sign is for it to be clear blood-red. If there is a thread-like line round it, one is likely to suffer troubles of long duration, before attaining happiness.

4. Ring finger. This is important as regards family and relatives, at least from the age of forty onwards. If bent, not lying close to middle finger, this means one will quarrel with a relative or lose spouse. It should be unblemished, and if there is no gap with the next fingers wealth in old age is assured. A line encircling this finger at the base is unlucky.

5. Little finger. If not bent, not blunt-tipped, even though it may be short, this is favourable; and a thread-like line encircling it indicates long life. But it would not be good for the other fingers to have similar circles. If the little finger tip is smaller than that of the ring finger that person will be intelligent, a good craftsman but rather poor.

The shell-bottom sign. This is very lucky if on all ten fingers. If it is on only one, that points to wealth; but to tiredness if on two, due to walking. If the sign is on 3, 4, 5, 6, 7 or 8 fingers this is a bad omen. On 9 it is good, but not so good as if on all ten.

Finger nails

They are attached to the bone and give valuable indications, which of course may be good or bad. If nails are thick, hard and sharp that person will be confident and brave, and can work without fear. If the nails are short or tender, he will be cunning and think only of self. He will also be uncertain and unlikely to complete work. If nails are long-pointed, he will be intelligent; and if thick and hard will live long. Blunt nails indicate stupidity; broken ones, disease. Good luck is foretold by nails being yellowish and lustrous. If nails are like a segmented tube, the owner will be a skilled craftsman; but if like the segments of a melon with crooked end, he will be a person who does not finish his work.

NOTES TO CHAPTER IV

1 *Khun Chang Khun Phan*, Trans. Prem Chaya, Book 2, p. 192, Bangkok, 1959.
2 Needham, op cit., p. 364. For an early Indian description of palm lines somewhat similar to the Chinese see Varāhamihira, loc.cit., pt. II, p. 65.
3 L.C. Arlington, 'Chinese versus Western Chiromancy', *China Journal*, 1927. The author is mainly concerned with establishing the supposed superiority of Western over Chinese methods. But he gives a useful bibliography of Chinese sources, and some of his quotations are very close to the Thai text utilized here.
4 Sangermano, op.cit., p. 147. Furthermore, in Bigandet's *Life of the Buddha*, Vol. I, p. 46, there is mention of a soothsayer's inspection of the infant Buddha's hand, at the time of his birth, foretelling his future greatness.
5 *B* III, pp. 88-108.
6 In the texts quoted by Arlington the mounts are identified with planets and each is influenced by one of the five elements.

CHAPTER V
MARRIAGE PARTNERS

The probing of one's fortune, and sometimes the help of a soothsayer in making up one's mind as to an immediate course of action, will be sure to yield pride of place in the minds of the young to the urgency of finding a suitable marriage partner. To begin with, of course, everyone knows those dangerous differences in age: 1, 2, 5 or 9 years, the couple will love each other like father and mother; 3, 4 or 6 years, like friends; 7, 8 or 10 years, will be likely to fight or quarrel. Most will not envisage the rest: 11, 12 or 13 years, likely to litigate; 14, 15 or 16 years, divorce likely; 17, 18 or 19 years, quarrel likely and the seeking of revenge.[1]

Birth elements

What many think cannot be overlooked is the compatability or otherwise of the birth element which governs every individual.[2] This, as we have seen, is the element associated with each year of the animal cycle, except that the metal mentioned is always iron, never gold. Now a favourable combination portends, in one word, happiness, to which wealth or rank is sometimes added. And as the majority of combinations are favourable it will be sufficient here to mention only those that are not. For these the outlook, if carried through, would by many be considered gloomy.

Male	Female
earth	water
earth	wood
wood	wood
wood	iron
fire	water
fire	earth
fire	wood
iron	fire

Birth animals

Despite the above, another treatise stresses rather the importance, of the respective animals of the birth years.[3] According to this a girl could obtain a forecast of her suitor's future position, that is if he married her. From our point of view it is of interest to set out the table in full, because this gives an illuminating picture of the range of social positions theoretically open to anyone of the freeman class, i.e. the majority of ordinary Thai people. The husband can even, as we shall see more fully later, be indeed a perfect angel *(devatā)*.

Partners' years of birth		Husband likely to be:
Rat +	Rat	Trader
	Ox	Royal teacher
	Tiger	Duck seller
	Hare	Rich man
	Large Snake	Boat hirer
	Small Snake (not good; should stop)	Fish trader
	Horse (good)	Army officer
	Goat	*Devatā*
	Monkey	Attap palm dealer
	Cock	Mahout
	Dog	Army officer
	Pig	Low official
Ox +	Ox	Rich man
	Tiger	Rewarded by king
	Hare	Treasury official
	Large snake	Noble
	Small snake	Low official
	Horse (good only later)	Mahout
	Goat	Rich man
	Monkey	Boatman
	Cock	Army officer
	Dog	Indra
	Pig	*Yakṣa*
Tiger +	Tiger	Soldier
	Hare	Junk (ship) trader.
	Large Snake	Junk officer

MARRIAGE PARTNERS

	Small Snake	Goldsmith
	Horse	Cook
	Goat	Boat hirer
	Monkey	Fishmonger
	Cock	Common person
	Dog	Official
	Pig	*Devatā*
Hare +	Hare	Rich man
	Large Snake	Farmer
	Small Snake	*Brahmā-devatā*
	Horse	Quarreler
	Goat	Cripple
	Monkey	Royal guru
	Cock	Army officer.
	Dog	Boat hirer (poor)
	Pig (difficult to rear children)	Spirit
Large Snake +	Large Snake	*Devatā*
	Small Snake	Rich man
	Horse	Low official
	Goat	Official
	Monkey	Indra
	Cock	Rice merchant
	Dog	Good companion
	Pig	Good companion
Small Snake +	Small Snake	Elephant keeper
	Horse	Rich man
	Goat	Noble
	Monkey	Good man
	Cock	*Devatā*
	Dog	Noble
	Pig	Commoner
Horse +	Horse	*Purohita* (royal chaplain)
	Goat	Noble
	Monkey	Rich man
	Cock	High official
	Dog	Treasury official
	Pig	Ne'er-do-well
Goat +	Goat	Village headman
	Monkey	Cattle grazier
	Cock	Fish dealer
	Dog	Robber chief
	Pig	Junk captain

Monkey +	Monkey (hard to rear children)	*Yakṣa*
	Cock	Kindly person
	Dog	Boat hirer
	Pig	Common person
Cock +	Cock (not good, should forbid)	Attap dealer
	Dog	Horse keeper
	Pig	Pig keeper
Dog +	Dog	Market overseer
	Pig (not constant)	Ne'er-do-well
Pig +	Pig	Deer stalker

From the above one may conclude that what a man makes of his life work depends in part on his wife, for had he married someone else his lot would have been different. For supporting evidence consider the success or otherwise of any entrepreneur couple in Bangkok.

Hostile Pairs

Fundamentally the question of marriage compatibility may be thought to depend on the theory of hostile pairs, as is the case also in Burma, this theory being originally a Chinese importation. A simple means of divination is popular for which a pair of entwined *nāgas* is needed, to the depiction of which the manuscripts often devote a good deal of artistic talent. Across them are marked a line of twelve small circles or numbers, two on the tail, middle and head of each *nāga*, each circle representing a year of age (Plate X).

Starting with the year of the Rat at the head, a man counts towards the tail; while a woman counts from the year of the Rat at the tail towards the head. And these are the omens:

If both end at head of the same *nāga*, excellent, they will live happily to an advanced age.
If each ends at the head of a different *nāga*, separation is likely.
If both end at the same *nāga*'s tail, very good, they will be happy.

ILLUSTRATIONS

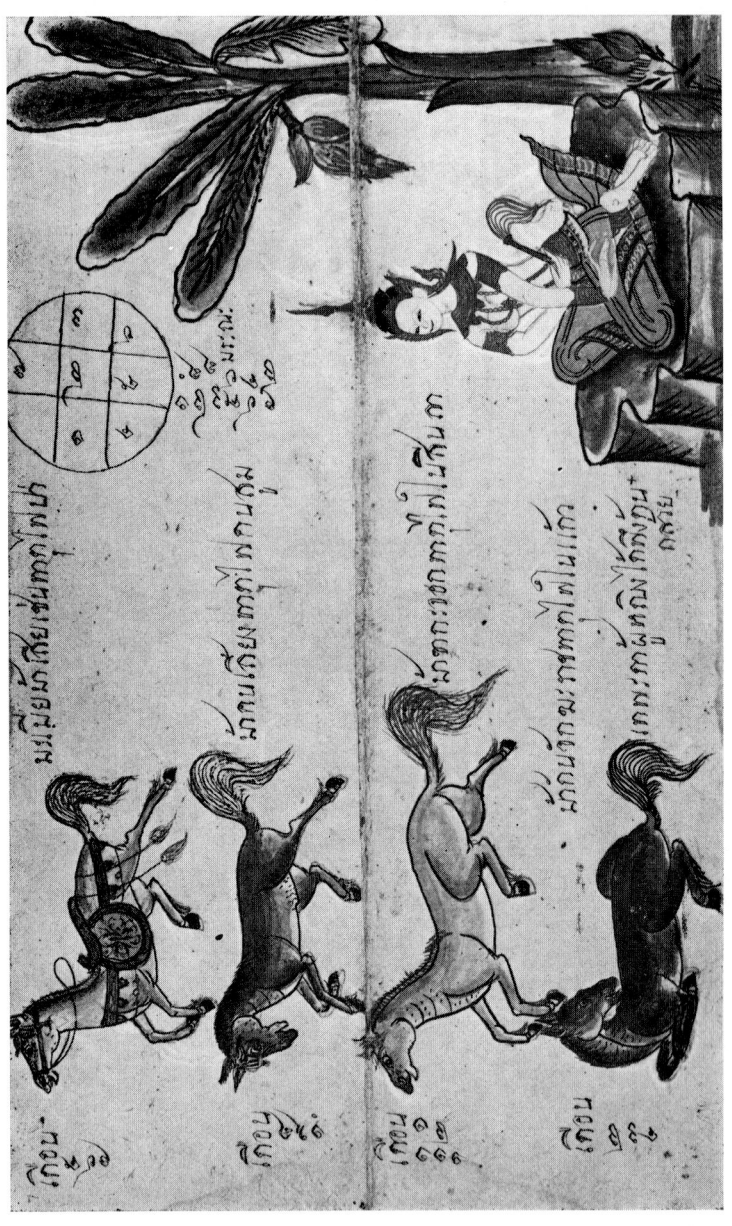

I. Year of the Horse

Reproduced by permission of the British Library. BL Or. 13650 f.7

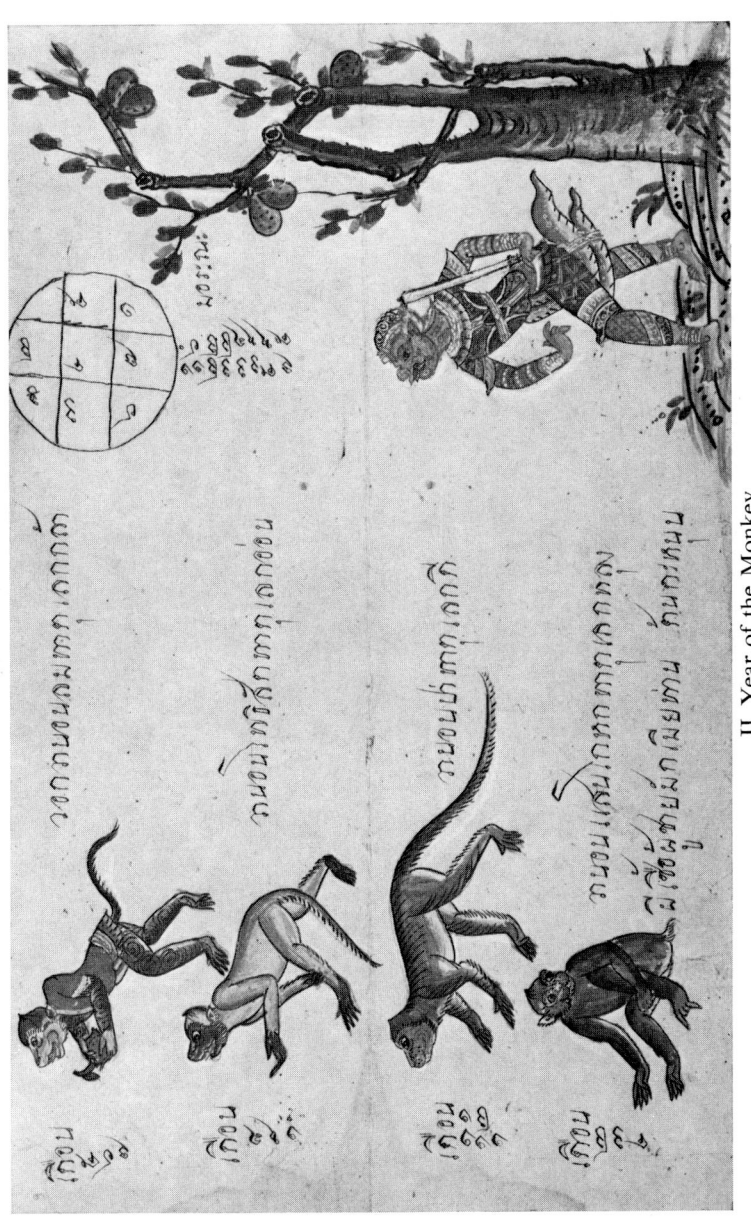

II. Year of the Monkey

Reproduced by permission of the British Library. BL Or. 13650 f.9

III. Year of the Rat
Reproduced by permission of the British Library. BL Or. 3593 f.3

IV. Year of the Ox
Reproduced by permission of the British Library. BL Or. 3593 f.5

V. Year of the Tiger
Reproduced by permission of the British Library. BL Or. 3593 f.7

VI. Year of the Small Snake
Reproduced by permission of the British Library. BL Or. 3593 f.10

VII. Year of the Monkey
Reproduced by permission of the British Library. BL Or. 3593 f.13

VIII. Year of the Dog
Reproduced by permission of the British Library. BL Or. 3593 f.23

IX. The so-called 'Signs of the Zodiac'
Reproduced by permission of the British Library. BL Or. 13650 f.25

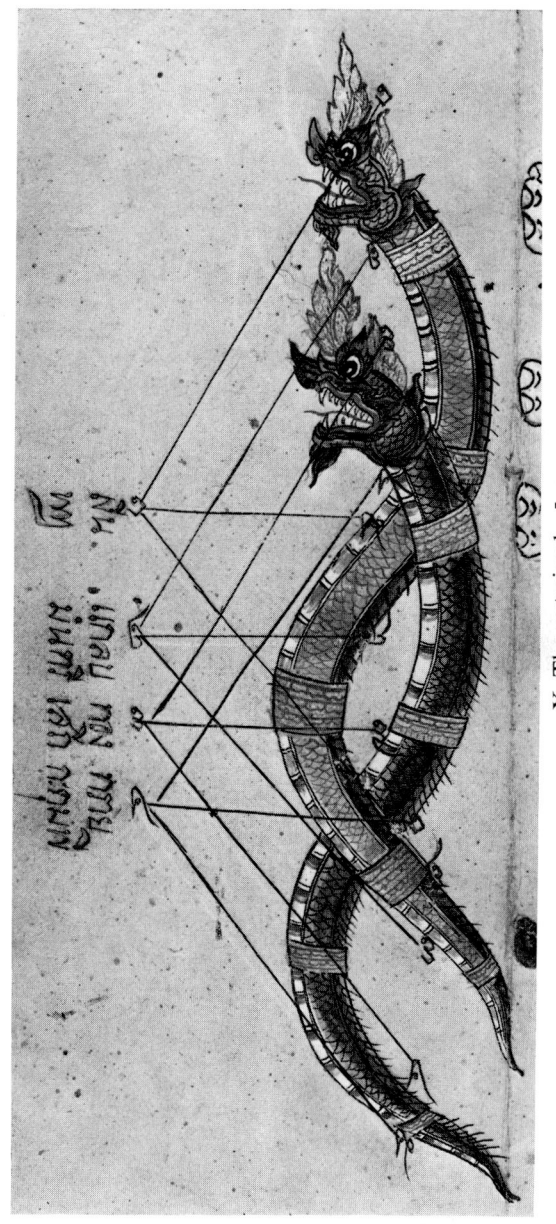

X. The entwined *nāgas*
Reproduced by permission of the British Library. BL Or. 13650 f.26

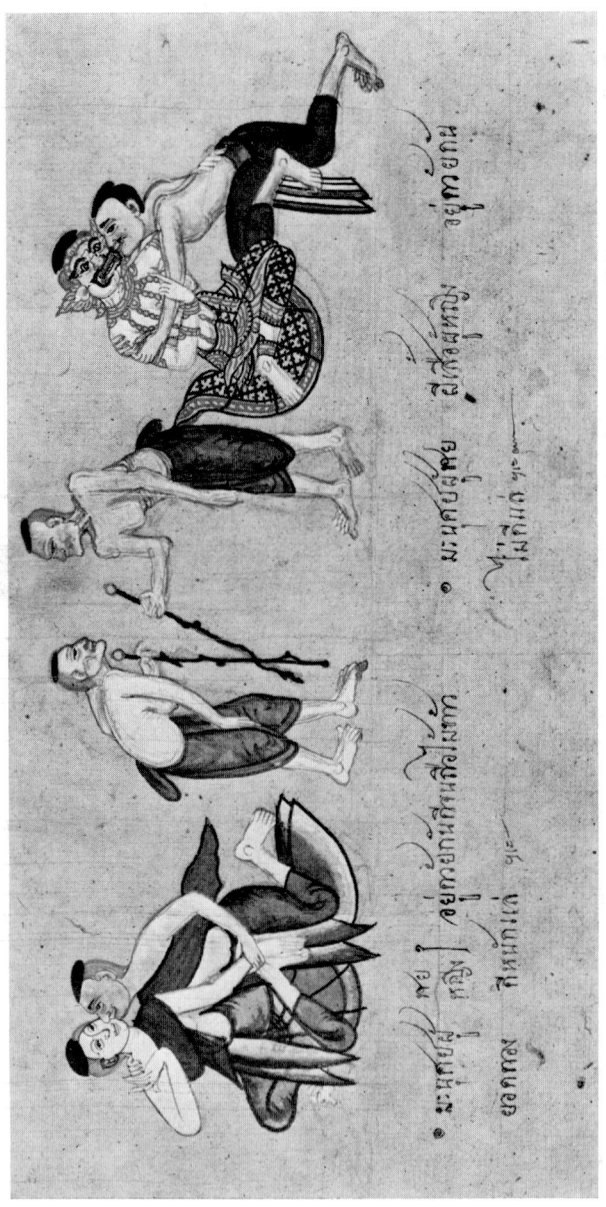

XI. A happy human marriage—a serene old age;
but if one marries a demoness . . .
Reproduced by permission of the British Library Bl Or. 3593 f.33

If each ends at a different *nāga*'s tail, not good. Divorce likely.
If both ends at the same *nāga*'s middle, very good, will be wealthy.
If each ends at a different *nāga*'s middle, not good, will separate.
If both end at head or tail of same *nāga*, moderately good.

If both end at the middle of the same *nāga*, with the same total of circles, this is not very good. They will agree at first, but trouble is likely to come.

If both end at the head, middle or tail of the same *nāga* with the same number of circles, this is not good; much sorrow.[4]

Some manuscripts add further portents by associating the *nāga* heads with wealth and the tails with poverty; while for the wife to end on the leading nāga's head would presage a hen-pecked husband. Sometimes a third *nāga* is entwined, to end up on the circles of which means infidelity on the part of one spouse or the other.

The manuscripts frequently show a drawing of a caparisoned elephant marked with figures as follows.[5] 1 on the head, 2 above the eye, 3 on the rump, 4 on belly, 5 on ear, 6 on mouth, 7 on tip of tail. The relative status of the position suggests the nature of the portents for the respective numbers obtained by adding the birth days and months (only) of the couple, totalling, then multiplying by 3 and dividing by 7. The portents for each possible remainder are as follows:

1, 2, or 4: good; much wealth, including elephants, horses, buffaloes, oxen and servants.

3: unable to get money and will experience much difficulty.

5: will be liable to quarrel with friends, but not seriously.

6: wealthy, but liable to quarrel.

7: unstable and likely to have poor reputation at first, but will improve after having children.[6]

The outlook—by remainders

Without the need of any intermediary such as the elephant drawing, the old treatises offer a number of variations of the remainder method by which the fortunes of a proposed marriage may be prognosticated.[7] So to know whether a couple will be happy one may add the numbers of the birth day, month and year of the animal cycle of each and then total the two. Multiply by 3 and divide by 7. Through the remainders the planetary deities inform us as follows: 1 and 2 poorly off; 3 and 5 will be rich; 6 will be great: elephants, horses and slaves in abundance; 4 will be so badly off as almost to have to sell the children; 0 or 7, worse, so will in fact have to sell them.

Another method: multiply the total present age of the couple by 3 and divide by 7. Remainders 1, 3, 7, 0 will separate, or lose money; 2, 4, 5 or 6 rich and happy and very devoted.

To know whether a couple will live to be old together: add the birth days, months and years of both, multiply by 3 and divide by 7. Remainders: 1, difficulties experienced for first three years, alternatively will die apart. 3, will die within a year, or if not will die apart during the first five years. 2, 4, 5 or 6 will gain money, elephants and horses and live together into old age.

To know which will die first: just add the years of both, multiply by 3 and divide by 7. Remainders: 1, 3, 7, 0 husband will die first; 2, 4, 5, 6 wife will die first.

A little more complicated: add the birth days, months and years of each together, and multiply by 9. Then place one above the other. Multiply the upper figure by 12 and the lower one by 3. Then divide each by 7. Remainders: 3, 2, 1, 0 not good, will dispute with relatives and friends; 4, 5, 6, 0 good, will be prosperous. If you change the upper and lower number round, it won't do any good.

Now as to source of future income: take the total ages, multiply by 3 and divide by 7. Remainders: 1, money from robbery; not lasting. 2, wealth of Indra, excellent. 3, the earnings of a fishwife. 4, dishonest money. 5, The wealth of a rich man. 6, A junk owner's wealth. 7 or 0, The earnings of a fisherman.

Mixed Marriages[8]

According to one well-known system marriages between men and women are likely to be favourable only with the following birth year couplets: Ox+Hare, Ox+Pig, Hare+Small Snake, Small

MARRIAGE PARTNERS

Snake + Pig. This is because for many people, perhaps the majority, mixed marriages are contemplated between humans of either sex, and partners who are actually *devatā* or demons (*yakṣa* or *yakṣī*) in disguise. This of course does not prevent the *devatā* and demons from sometimes marrying their own kind; and since none are immortal, but were all born somewhere at some time, all are subject to the fortunes dictated by year of birth. All this may seem incomprehensible to many of us, but is second nature to the ordinary Thai who has been nourished on the *Rāmakien* and similar literature during childhood.

A male and female *devatā* will live together very happily and have many children, provided that the couples are Rat + Horse, Rat + Goat, Large Snake + Goat, or Large Snake + Horse. Such will also be the case with a *yakṣa* and a *yakṣī*, though apt to quarrel at times, if the couples are Tiger + Cock, Monkey + Dog, or Cock + Monkey; but Tiger + Monkey and Dog + Cock are only moderately satisfactory, while with Tiger + Dog disputes gain the upper hand.

Now in the mixed field for a man to marry a female *devatā* is excellent, though liable to temporary separation—of which examples in the literature are known to every Thai. But this satisfactory state of things depends on the couples being Ox + Horse, Ox + Goat, or Large Snake + Goat. On the other hand marriage between a woman and a *devatā* is generally good, there will be children though the pair are liable to quarrel and part. Best are Rat + Hare and Large Snake + Hare, while Rat + Pig and Large Snake + Pig are moderately favourable. A *devatā* marrying a *yakṣī* can only be moderately good (mainly in the case of Rat + Tiger), for they will have children who will not respect them. A *yakṣa* marrying a female *devatā* will have some children, but being apt to quarrel they will get on together only moderately. For them the only couplets at all favourable are Cock + Horse, Monkey + Horse and Cock + Goat.

A woman may suitably marry a *yakṣa*, but it is bad if they part (like Kumbhanda and Kesa Sumanda in the *Rāmakien*). The most favourable are Monkey + Hare, Monkey + Pig and Cock + Hare. Lastly, it is claimed that the marriage of a man with a *yakṣī* will sometimes be happy but is equally likely to end in hatred, so the prospects cannot be more than moderate (Plate XI). At first all may go well, but later there will be separation, as with Nang Meri and Phra Rot in the popular Thai story. The most hopeful are Ox+Tiger, Ox+Dog, Small Snake+Tiger, Small Snake+Dog, and Dog+Pig.

'How can I *know* if my fiancé is a *yakṣa*?' a sophisticated young lady in Bangkok recently asked me, with more than a trace of anxiety. 'Only if his hair is curly and his eyes are slightly redder than normal' I replied, reminding her of several passages in Thai literature. She seemed relieved.

NOTES TO CHAPTER V

1 *B* I, p. 54.
2 *B* I, pp. 52 ff.
3 *B* III, pp. 50–52. I have not found that the years are ever considered incompatible on any supposition of natural enmity of the species, such as tiger and dog, as is stated in an article said to be chiefly translated from Siamese MSS, 'How the respectable and affluent among the Siamese arrange for the marrying of their children', *Bangkok Calendar*, 1864, p. 75 f.
4 *B* I, p. 55 f.
5 Or somewhat differently, as in the Satow MS, folio 41.
6 *BSMB* p. 487.
7 *BSMB* pp. 198 ff.
8 *B* III, pp. 50–70. Interspersed are allusions which might bear a homosexual interpretation. If so, possibly it is the text that is corrupt.

CHAPTER VI

A HOME OF ONE'S OWN

As elsewhere in this world of ever-growing population, the Thai young couple will want to set up a home of their own, and in due course, with a family to accommodate, will want to possess a larger one. Traditionally the bridal house should be established in the compound of the bride's parents. These with relatives and friends would give much assistance, the timber and attap formerly being readily available. This is still largely the custom in agricultural communities where there is adequate land.[1] But the timber has probably to be bought, and some of the labour has to be hired. Complex rituals should be carried out, and a great many omens taken heed of. This applies not only to the building of a house but equally to monks' quarters in a *wat*, the temple buildings themselves, a law court, an eating house, a cattle shed or a stable.

How far are such practices maintained to-day? I am told that even in Bangkok it is often considered vital to go through the ritual motions of erecting the main posts, even though the posts cannot actually be used in the construction. In the rural communities, therefore, it is reasonable to suppose, that the ancient traditions are still quite well maintained. Certainly for the north we have a valuable account of such house-building as recorded by a well-known religious scholar resident in Chiengmai.[2] His careful description indicates that the practices there, though not exactly the same as those of the central Thai treatise which I follow, are a near variant. And the author shows himself to be possessed of good anthropological judgement when he writes: 'Although in the opinion of some modern groups, these practices are nonsensical, they do have a value for the believer. They give him confidence and thereby bring good fortune, and also dispose his mind towards things which are good and beneficial.'

Many young Thais cannot wait to know whether their future venture in house building will be successful or not. There is a way to find out. Just write down those powerful seven numbers, for

A HOME OF ONE'S OWN 73

day, month and year of birth in three tiers as on page 29; and distinguish each column by a letter as in Fig 6.

	A	B	C	D	E	F	G
Day	o	o	o	o	o	o	o
Month	o	o	o	o	o	o	o
Year	o	o	o	o	o	o	o

Fig. 6

Then total up each column, but use only those of 10 or more. Next write them on the given elevation sketch (Fig. 7), but put a cross instead of a figure if the figure is below 10. Connect up the numbers by lines, but do not connect the crosses or the crosses to numbers.

If the model can be completed you'll have a very good house, one in a hundred. If only one number is missing it will still be a good house and you will live happily in it. If the building is incomplete but is put in a firm position you can live there quite well. If that is not the case it is inauspicious; you will have trouble and probably have to abandon it. If the model has only one post, that is no good; two are sufficient but three are better. If roofing or beams, or even only beams, are lacking, it is useless to have walls. If the walls are lacking the floor is of no value. If there's only one post in the ground, a good roof won't do; if the roof is lacking posts are no good. In short, if the model represents a house—good; if it does not—no good.[3]

The Thai treatise on building construction bears the stamp of venerable antiquity. It is of Indian origin and stems ultimately from such rules as were laid down by Varāhamihira.[4] But what we actually have is closely paralleled by Burmese practices;[5] less so by the regulations laid down in the Sinhalese *Māyāmataya*,[6] itself a translation of a much older Sanskrit work, and indeed already adumbrated by Varāhamihira. Here we shall need to concern ourselves only with the Thai treatise.[7]

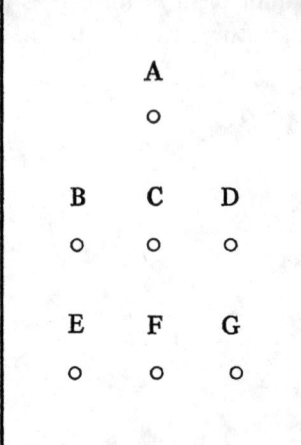
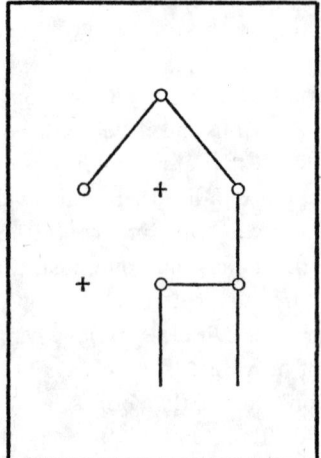
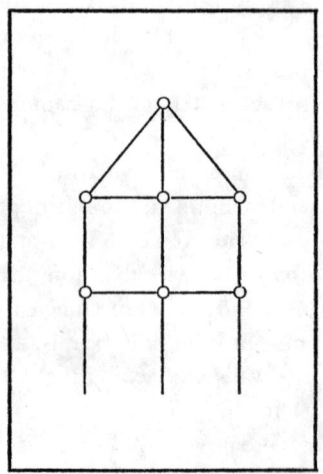

Fig. 7

A HOME OF ONE'S OWN

In selecting a suitable site attention should first be given to the proximity of any high ground, even a white-ant hill. If such should stand to the E., S., S.W., N.W., N., or N.E. the portent is favourable, mainly taking the form of wealth and prosperity. On the other hand such elevations being on the S.E. or W. are unfavourable, fire burning the house, or wife and children giving trouble.

Then it is essential to test the portents of the ground. One should first taste a sample of the soil: acid, insipid, sweet or very sweet. The test should be made during the first, second or third months. Dig a small hole in the northern part of the area, and lay some fresh banana leaves on the exposed soil. Pile a heap of fresh and clean thatch grass *(Imperata cylindrica)* over them. Let the banana leaves stay one night in contact with the earth, until its exudation adheres to them. Then taste them. If the taste is bitter it is an acid place, and would be a source of trouble and danger. If the taste is sweet it is moderately good, and the place can be used. If it is insipid it is good and auspicious; you will live there in complete happiness. But for the taste to be very sweet would be ill-omened. One will do well to follow this advice, insists the treatise.

However, if you prefer to use the sense of smell you may do so. Just dig a deep ditch and smell the earth from it. If it has a smell like a lotus or *Orthocarpus siamensis,* the site is excellent, a real Brahman place. If it smells of Jack fruit or Jasmine or a 'perfect' white lotus it is good, and fortune will attend you. A bad smell is, of course, ill-omened.

There is still another method, which gives a little more trouble but is highly recommended. Take one new laid hen's egg, with three gold leaves and red, green, yellow, white and black cotton. Put them in a new pot and close the mouth with several folds of white cloth. Then dig a hole about two cubits deep, bury the pot and fill in with earth. Thirty days later dig it up. If the objects are still good and clean, that place is most propitious, one in a hundred or a thousand. If it turns out like that it is because of one's merit. If, however, the egg is putrid, and the gold and cotton are not as clean as before, provided that the earth tastes insipid you can live there and enjoy good fortune.˙ Only if the cotton colours have changed and the earth tastes very sweet or bitter you cannot safely live there.

Now consider the shape of the plot. If it is perfectly round like the moon you can live there happily, triumph over your enemies and enjoy peace of mind. Other favourable shapes are those of a cut lime, a junk or a square. But if the square is imperfect through one side being too wide, or one corner is cut off or eaten into, there would be trouble. If one side has two corners eaten into, but there is a compensatory promontory projecting between them, you can live there in permanent bliss. Even better if the middle of one side of the square is eaten into, but the two corners of that side project, so that it is shaped like a pair of trousers. Surprisingly, should the place be shaped like a flag of victory, that is to say triangular, the outlook is bad: the occupier would suffer punishment.[8]

Having decided that the character of the plot is favourable, the question arises as to when it would be auspicious to start work. Should the preliminaries have been completed already in the first lunar month, one could start straight away; but not so if you are already into the third month. This, together with the fifth, seventh, eighth, tenth and eleventh months are considered unfavourable, and hold in store calamities of all kinds for the transgressor. So one should make a beginning in any of the remaining months, the twelfth being especially recommended. Not only would you then have two excellent months before you but it is for the twelfth alone that is explicitly held out 'an abundance of wealth, elephants, horses, cattle, buffaloes and slaves, both male and female.' As to deciding the day on which to start work there is no difficulty. One simply bears in mind that the planets of the cardinal points, Moon, Mercury, Jupiter and Venus are favourable, while those of the sub-cardinal, Sun, Mars and Saturn are not. So avoid Sunday, Tuesday and Saturday, with their portents of fever, bloodshed and, of course, the house being burnt down.

Everything centres around the erection of the main posts. The timber for these should be prepared during the months one to four so, unless there had been considerable foresight, delay on this score can be envisaged. The posts should never be irregular. Those that are of the same diameter all through (male) are the best, though those smaller at one end (female) can be used. It is most important to observe what knots are visible in each post. If they are 1, 3, 5 or 7 in number the portent is favourable, one will be prosperous and defeat one's enemies. The other numbers up to nine augur danger and such posts should be discarded.[9] However certain large-scale distribution of knots, at beginning and end, or small and widely scattered, called rats' breasts, are very lucky. A post with worm-eaten or mouldy knots should be avoided.

Fortunately, to avoid much waste of timber and labour, ill-omened posts can be treated so as to change them into serviceable ones. Bad knots can be cut out and the holes filled with a mixture of turnip, nutmeg, red cow's dung, honey and milk, one part of each. Then paint the ill-omened posts with a mixture consisting of equal parts of eagle-wood, red orpiment, mosaic gold, cow's milk and honey. The posts immediately become favourable.

When cutting the timber, attention should be paid to the direction in which each trunk falls. For it to fall to the S.E., S., N.W., W. or N. would be ill-omened, and would indicate at the least fire burning the house or robbers breaking in, at the worst the death of the owner. A fall to the E. is good, one to the S.W. will assure good sons, while chief honours are accorded to the N.E. which should provide the coveted elephants, horses, cattle, buffaloes and slaves both male and female. One cannot omit to mention, though one is here in the realm of magic rather than divination, that the selected principal posts are now given names, such as Brahmā, Diamond, Happy, which should be written on cards to be attached to each post by a virgin. The posts are then wrapped in cloth of appropriate colours.

Before one can start to dig the pits for planting the posts one has to consider the position of the Śeṣa Nāga for that time of year. This is the case at the start of many important undertakings and is common to all those parts of Southeast Asia where there has been Indian influence. The Śeṣa Nāga is the great serpent which supports the three worlds and moves its head, following the sun, a degree every day. So in the 4th, 5th and 6th months the Nāga's head faces W., his tail is to the E., his belly is to the S., and his back to the N. So you must dig to the S., throw the earth to the

S.E., and raise the chief post facing in that direction. Similarly, with due variation, for the other three-monthly periods as the Nāga moves round. The point is that so long as you dig towards the Nāga's belly the portents will be favourable. If you dig a pit and raise a post facing the Nāga's head the mother of the family will die first, if towards its tail, children, wife and slaves will run away, if towards its back the owner will be ill. Before digging, for the quarter above-mentioned, offerings of yellow cloth, popcorn, flowers, candles etc. should be made to the Nāga and a short Sanskrit spell should be pronounced. For the other three quarters the cloth should be black, red or white respectively.[10]

When work is being started on the house one should note the direction of a rainbow or of any of the following animals approaching: vulture, turtle dove, ibis, egret, kite, snake or bee. The omens are good if they come from W., N.W., N., or N.E., the opposite if they come from the other directions. In that case the omens would range from fire burning, robbers attacking or the death of the owner. If someone should happen to bring flesh, liver or a dead mammal near the construction site, that means the owner will gain in property; and if the meat-bearing stranger should come from the N. or S. that indicates gold and a happy future. On the other hand a person coming from the W. indicates defeat and one bringing fire indicates the owner will suffer from fever. One coming from the N.W. and wearing flowers behind the ears and a red garment is another sign that the house will be burnt. As some may regret to learn, a cat coming from the N.W. signifies that robbers will attack.

While pits for the minor posts may be dug by anyone, that does not apply to those for the chief ones. To dig these special spades must be provided with *Cassa* and *Shorea* wood handles, and men should be found named Indra, Brahmā, Victory or Crystal. They are likely to assure good fortune. However much depends on any lucky or unlucky objects they may uncover, though the bad omens can usually be averted. Gold and silver objects, stone, metal ore or tin, or traces of a blindworm, are all welcome signs pointing to prosperity and happiness. But iron is a bad sign, indicating that the owner will not long enjoy good health: one must take lotus flowers and water that has washed the feet of a gold image, with which to sprinkle the pit, then all will be well. Another ill-omened discovery would be long-jointed bamboo, such as those used for blowpipes. To avert the omen one must get monks to come and chant, also sprinkle the place with holy water. The finding of bones would necessitate sprinkling the pits with holy water in which crystal, gold and silver rings had been dipped. Almost equally unwelcome finds are signs of former occupation, such as string, rice husks, bricks and rats' leavings, to neutralize which honey and holy water must be sprinkled. Copper and wood found together indicate a lawsuit.

Once the main posts are raised it may be difficult to keep them absolutely upright, so Fate now has an excellent opportunity to indicate the outlook. Actually most directions are fortunate—or the house never would be built—but should they lean to E., W., or N. the signs are gloomy; should, as is most unlikely, one actually fall to the E. or W., that signifies respectively the burning of the house and the death of the owner. The treatise seems to suggest that to assure happiness there is no objection to helping the chief post to lean a little to the North-east. To encourage it to stay that way one should take five gold leaves, three banana leaves, and one sugar cane, and bind them firmly to the top of the post. Offerings of leaf platters of rice and also candles should be placed at the base.

Much advice of a definitely practical character is given to the builders, which does not concern us here. Sufficient to mention that with a stilted building the storey should be the same height as the supporting stilts. If it is higher, defeat for the owner is presaged; if lower, he will lose money. For a house door add the proposed breadth and height, multiply by three and divide by eight: if the remainder is 1, 2, 3 or 7 you are on the right lines, but if it is 4, 5, 6 or 0 you will lose money. A breadth of five feet is ideal. A verandah door should only be $3\frac{1}{2}$ feet broad; if wider the portent is for fire to burn the house. A ladder door should be just over 4 feet wide: any wider will invite illness and poverty. A gate should face E., N.E., or N. to ensure happiness; one towards the S.E. means ruin.

I cannot refrain from ending with a little magic, which is brought to bear on the situation when the ladder is finally put up to the door: If the ladder is on the north, have gold taken up first; if on the east, first take up a gold and silver garment; if on the north-west, a cat is now welcome.

No home is complete without a garden, so the Thais have always traditionally thought, and moreover it should basically be planted with auspicious trees. In this they are following the example set by ancient India, for Varāhamihira already counselled 'Plant in the garden or by the house, in the first place, auspicious trees, as Ariṣṭa, Aśoka, Rottleria, Siris and Priyangu-trees'. [11]Thai treatises offer two alternative schemes for such planting of auspicious trees around a centre.[12] The planting of the trees at the cardinal and sub-cardinal points would appear to incorporate the concept of the microcosm, though whether this was ever conscious cannot be stated.

		Coconut		
Bale tree or Metum (*Aegle marmelos*)	N.E.	E.	S.E.	Lacquer tree (*Melanorrhoea*)
Tamarind	N.	Centre	S.	Mango
Ixora coccina (ornamental shrub with red flowers)	N.W.	W.	S.W.	Jack
		Phutsa (*Zizyphus jujuba*)		

Alternative plan:

		Bamboo		
Rattan (*Milia*)	N.E.	E.	S. E.	Saraphi (*Orthocarpus siamensis*)
Bale or Metum	N.	Centre	S.	Mango
Phutsa	N. W.	W.	S. W.	Phikun (*Mimusops elugi*)
		Jack		

Fig. 8.

These directions as to what should be grown are usefully complemented by the information published by Phya Anuman as to the trees which Thais would *not* plant in their house compounds by reason of their unlucky nature.[13] Such taboos are still generally adhered to, and they are often based on the inauspicious associations of the names. Thus the *Tau Rang (Caryota mitis-palmae)*, an ornamental palm, is not admitted because the word *rang* has also the meaning of deserted or abandoned. Similarly with the *Sala* and *Rakam* trees *(Zallaca)* whose Thai names mean respectively forsaken and affliction; but the gardeners are happy to use them for hedges since their sharp spines deter trespassers. The *Sok* tree *(Saraka indica)* may be the same as the Indian Asoka, Phya Anuman opined, but whereas in Sanskrit the name had the auspicious meaning sorrowless, in Thai *sok* has come to mean just the opposite. Again the Thai name for Frangipani, *lanthom*, too closely resembles *rathom* = agony. Some trees have unlucky spirit associations, but may be found in monastery compounds, sometimes associated with ghost stories. It is interesting to note that *Phutsa*, the Indian jujube tree, which is recommended by our treatise to be grown on the west, is not now wanted in gardens. Certainly its flowers have a nauseous smell, but the reason it is now thought unlucky, Phya Anuman supposed, is that the last syllable *sa* of its name also means 'to diminish', and this could have an adverse effect on the occupier's fortunes.

Returning to our treatise, this is not only concerned, as one might suppose, with making the garden a happy microcosm by planting the right trees at the key points. It also lays down rules for the proper days and times for planting successfully all those luscious fruits and vegetables which the rich soil of the Menam valley can produce so bountifully.[14]

Sunday: Plant ginger, *Alpinia galangas* (aromatic rhizomes), Curcuma, Turmeric and yams—*at night*.
Monday: Plant fruit trees in general and sugar cane—*at night*.
Tuesday: Plant Basil *(Ocimum)* and coriander—*when the sun is well up*.
Wednesday: Plant handsome flowering shrubs of various kinds.

Thursday: Plant long pumpkins, water melons, gourds, Indian corn, beans and sesame.

Friday: Plant trees, to have beautiful branches, leaves and fruit.

Saturday: Plant trees, *when the sun is well up*, to get good leaves; *in the morning*, to get fruit; *in the evening*, to get roots.

The idea governing Saturday's instruction finds fuller expression in the recommendation to plant on Sunday for roots, Monday for stems, Tuesday for branches, Wednesday for flowers, Thursday for fruits, Friday for seeds and Saturday for leaves.[15]

For the more traditionally minded Thais the daily round of home life involves giving due attention to the proper days for carrying out a multitude of domestic and personal chores. Slave buying was removed from the list a century ago. Sunday, Wednesday and Saturday were the auspicious days; Monday invited illness; Tuesday litigation; while Thursday's and Friday's purchases would simply run away. However, one should still avoid donning new clothes on Tuesday or Saturday, and should only do any sewing on Wednesday, Thursday and Friday. Hair may not be washed or cut safely on Monday and Wednesday, while nails should not be cut on Tuesday, Thursday and Saturday if sorrow is to be avoided and prosperity achieved.[16]

I understand that rats and mice are, no less than formerly, inclined to gnaw garments when opportunity offers, and this is lucky only if it occurs on Sunday, Monday or Friday.[17] But perhaps greater importance is attached to the shape of the holes made in the cloth by the rodents. Examples are: shape of coconut shell measure—wealth; lotus flower—happiness; a new moon—make offerings then all will be well; dog's footprint—will become a noble; chank shell—success in every way.[18] For the animal to bite a part of the person is most ill-omened. This was known to Bastian who specified that nibbling a person's hair indicated that his parents were doomed, a bite in the back foretold loss of property, in the hand trouble to the family, in the left leg trouble for a friend.[19]

When leaving the house, and I don't mean necessarily for a major journey, but just to call on a neighbour, go to the village, or inspect the padi fields, it is as well to keep an eye open for the omens. So a gecko lizard calling or a person sneezing in front, on the left, or on one's path, are encouraging, but if behind, on the right, or above, one might do well to pause. Similarly animals moving from left to right, leading one on, or coming from behind, presage good fortune, while contrary movements are ill-omened. Unfamiliar encounters on one's outdoor excursion should not be ignored, especially it would seem if one is not in a very good mood. If then you happen to meet a man armed with a spear and sword and go along with him that would be an ill-omened thing to do. Or you may meet a relative on the way and accompany him somewhere. If he turns unpleasant and some cattle bar the way, that would be inauspicious, equally so if you see a dark woman on the track.[20]

If one chooses to stay quietly at home, sitting with friends or relatives in front of the house, beneath a shady tree, or very pleasantly beneath the covered landing stage beside the river or canal, there is no certain freedom from supernatural intimations. Indeed it is often just the time for them. There is always a chance that a small bird, lizard, bat, beetle, spider or butterfly may happen to fall among the company—but of course I should not have used the word chance. It is indeed a bad omen for someone present if it falls dead, for it means that that person will lose a relative.

For someone sitting at home alone, the fallen animal can have more varied significance. If it falls on the left it means the death of a relative, but money coming if it falls on the right arm or hand. A quarrel is indicated if it falls on the left arm. On the left breast of a woman it portends a husband, on the right of a man a handsome wife, on his stomach wealth, and on hers a baby. For the animal to fall on a man's ear, it means he must fear a woman; on his left foot, he will receive agreeable news, but danger if on his right. The animal may be alive. In that case, should it quickly crawl on to one's head that is an excellent omen, but if on to the body it heralds relatives' bad intentions. However, if it climbs on to one's shoulders, wealth is coming; and if one happens to be a pretty woman—every kind of happiness. Being wild, it is much more likely to run or fly away as quickly as it can. In that case one must watch the direction: East means that robbers will break in, S.E. trouble from friends, and W. from relatives. However S.W., N.W., and N.E. are portents of coming good fortune.

An involunatry twitch is a sign that has perhaps been almost universally considered of divinatory significance; and perhaps nowhere more catalogued in detail than by the Thais and, I may add, the Malays. For the former a twitch on the right shoulder means the loss of money and valued possessions, and on the left an angry dispute. So it is interesting to note that legend makes Hang Tueh, a hero of mediaeval Malacca, wear his magic keris on a day when just such a twitch on his right shoulder had led him to expect a brawl.[21] Very likely the Thai and Hindu Malays had both derived their lists from a similar Indian source. Not all the Thai twitches reveal the association of ideas so closely as the one on the right cheek which presages money coming from a beloved, and the one on the left cheek which means happiness with the beloved. It will be enough to classify roughly, but not exhaustively, a few examples:

Wealth coming: Behind the right eye, corner of right eye, left ear, right nipple, near lips, right hand, right knee, left armpit.

Beloved thinking of, or letter coming from, etc.: Left eye, middle of eye, behind left palm, ring finger, base of nipples, left wrist, chest, left forearm, right toes.

Family relations, good or bad: neck, right forearm, corner of left eye, left knee, left foot, right toes, chin.

Bad news, disputes etc.: right ear, below eye, nose, right arm-pit, index, middle and little fingers, right wrist.

Distant travel: right arm (fortunate), right foot and left toes.[22]

NOTES TO CHAPTER VI

1. J. H. Kemp, 'Initial Marriage in Rural Thailand', *In Memoriam Phya Anuman Rajadhon*, Bangkok, 1970, pp. 73–85.
2. Sanguan Chotisukharat, 'Supernatural Beliefs and Practices in Chiengma ', *Journ. of the Siam Society*, Vol. 59. pt. 1, 1971, pp. 211–233.
3. *B* II, pp. 49–51.
4. Varāhamihira, Chap. LIII.
5. Sangermano, op. cit., p. 143; Scott, op. cit., pp. 76f.
6. Partially translated by A.K. Coomaraswamy, *Mediaeval Sinhalese Art*, 2nd. edn., New York, 1956, pp.120–128; *Le Purana Māyāmataya*, French trans. by Jinadasa Liyanaratne, *Pub. EFEO*, Tome CIX, 1976.
7. *B* I, pp. 94–106; II, pp. 87 f. III, pp. 79f. Additionally there are comprehensive accounts (in Thai) on traditional housebuilding, largely based on the Thai treatise in Anuman Rajadhon, *Praḥbenī, nöang näi kan plūkröan*, Bangkok, 1964, and Urakhin Wiriyabūrana, *Praḥbenī Thai chapap braḥ mahārājagrū*, Bangkok, 1969. B.J.Terwiel, op. cit., Chap. VII, gives a general account of the proceedings as seen in a central Thailand village.
8. In India a triangular (or five-sided) plot for building is to be avoided, being associated with finality, according to J. Abbott, *The Keys of Power*, London, 1932, p. 300.
9. Thus it is definitely stated in our text, but it may be that Sangermano's Burmese source is nearer the common original when he states that the Burmese divide certain timbers into ten compartments and observe in which a knot occurs (loc. cit.). This receives support from what we shall see later as to Thai beliefs concerning the indications of knots in boats.
10. The injunction against facing the Nāga includes travel, seeing a sick person (if patient is to recover), laying a wager, looking for lost objects, and going to war. When a 90° movement daily of the Nāga through the cardinal and sub-cardinal points is mentioned this must be ascribed to a local misunderstanding, due to the over-ruling influence of the planets (e.g. *B* III, pp. 77f.)
11. Varāhimihira, II, p. 37.3.
12. *B* II, pp. 85 f.
13. Phya Anuman Rajadhon, 'Some Siamese Superstitions about Trees and Plants', *Journ. of the Siam Society*, Vol. 49, pt. 1, 1961, pp. 57–63. Similarly *BSMB* p. 475.
14. *B* II, p. 86.
15. *B* II, p. 81.
16. ibid. Contrariwise in the West we have 'Cut them on Tuesday, cut them for health; cut them on Thursday, a new pair of shoes; cut them on Saturday, see sweetheart tomorrow'. (And, of course, 'cut them on Sunday, cut them for evil, the whole of the week you'll be ruled by the devil.')
17. *B* II, p. 81.

18 The Malays also draw omens from the gnawing by mice of mats, pillows and coats. See R.O.Winstedt, *The Malay Magician*, London, 1951, p. 91.
19 Bastian, op. cit., p. 490.
20 *B* II, p. 68.
21 R.O.Winstedt, loc.cit.
22 Summarized from *BSMB*, pp. 504 ff.

CHAPTER VII

AGRICULTURE AND TRADE

Agriculture has always been the mainstay of the Thai economy, and for most of the country this means almost entirely rice cultivation. The expansion of fruit gardening around Bangkok, and the introduction of a number of subsidiary crops during recent years, has scarcely dented the predominance of the padi field. Apart from the officials and the fishermen the vast majority of the rural working population has always been engaged in the production of Thailand's staple crop.

For no other crop is ample water a greater essential. While much has been done of recent decades to bring more land under profitable production through the improvement of irrigation, and above all by the construction of vast dams, the need is still felt for a good monsoon, and anxiety persists that the rains may be inadequate. Certainly complete failure is scarcely known, but there is nevertheless all the difference between too little, enough and, it may even be, too much. Supposing that the young couple, now settled in their new home, belong to an average fairly well-off rural family, beyond the garden they will have padi lands of their own to till, and the promise of the rains will be a more lively consideration for them than it ever was before. Here are a few of the methods of prognostication made available by the textbooks, some of them used by the Brahmans in their official forecasts.

One apparently ancient system which was formerly included among those employed by the Brahmans in predicting the harvest at New Year has, according to a note in the earlier edition of our printed treatise, been abandoned.[1] According to this the *nāgas*, who provide the rain, do so in varying numbers and varying amounts according to the year of the animal cycle. And in each year we are told the amounts to be expected early, middle and late in the rainy season. But when it is stated that in the Year of the Hare, when there are only two *nāgas* engaged, the rainfall will be good throughout, whereas in the Year of the Dog, with the maximum number of seven *nāgas* functioning, rainfall will only be good in the middle and late season, it is not surprising that doubts should have arisen.

Many farmers may well be content to put their trust in the signs of the heavens, which are both varied and explicit. They show themselves already in the third month (February), the height of the dry season, when we are advised to make our observations.[2]

Moon. On the third waxing, third month, look at the moon. If the horns appear equal that means that rice that year will be cheap, and all will eat well. But if the moon appears to lean to the north, rains will be delayed everywhere in the rainy season, but the crop will be a little better in the north. If it leans to the south, this means that there will be less rain in the north, and rice there will be a little dearer.

Clouds. The sky is by no means always cloudless during the dry season, and occasionally one may have a 'mango shower.' If on the third of the waxing, third month, clouds come up very dark that means that rainfall will be ample, rice abundant and everyone happy. But if clouds come up red from the north and south together that means little water, rice dear, much illness and—the danger of war.

Mango showers. If there is a heavy shower in the third month, and also sunshine, that year the rains will be good and ploughing easy. But if there is scarcely a shower it is a bad omen for agriculture. Should, however, the sky appear red in both the N.W. and the W. it will soon rain. But if the wind blows from N. to S. and from S. to N. there will be news of war.

Thunder. A charming set of portents. From the first night of the third month you should listen for thunder and in the fourth month you should listen for fifteen days from the fifth night of the waxing to the fourth of the waning. After that date predictions would be invalid. Now this system is predicated on the existence of gates at the cardinal and sub-cardinal points of the heavens, also at the zenith, each of which is guarded by a *devatā*. And whichever gate is opened will determine the quality of the water supply subsequently to be vouchsafed to the Thai people. The gate to be opened is indicated by the direction in which thunder is heard during the approved period.

So if it thunders to the E. the *devatā* concerned will open the

Wind Gate: rice, beans and sesame will be abundant—but many people will be taken ill.

If it thunders to the S.E. the *devatā* will open the Gold Gate: that year the rains will be ample, rice and all foodstuffs plentiful.

If it thunders to the S. it will be the Fire Gate: people will suffer and smallpox will rage.

If it thunders to the S.W. it will be the Stone Gate: the rains will be good, rice and fish abundant; but many people will be ill and there will be strife.

If it thunders to the W. the *devatā* will open the Iron Gate: this means that though the rains and harvest will be good, there will be much illness about, and also strife and oppression.

If it thunders to the N.W. it will be the Silver Gate: there will be plenty of water, but many people will die; crops good in some parts, bad in others.

If it thunders to the N. it will be the Water Gate: There will be too much water and the land will be submerged, with consequent loss of crops.

If it thunders to the N.E. the *devatā* will open the Earth Gate: rains adequate, rice, beans and sesame crops good, and everyone contented.

If it thunders above, Brahmā himself will open the Heaven Gate and two other *devatā* will open two other good gates, the result being that the rains will be just right. Rice, beans and sesame will abound. People will eat well and happiness prevail throughout the land of the Thai.

Now we come to a relatively sophisticated system which used to be promulgated officially at New Year and requires a little calculation.[3] You take the year of the Chula era,[4] subtract 4 and then divide by 7. If the remainder is 1 the planetary deity concerned is Sun or Saturn who provides that 400 showers will fall over the whole of the middle world, proportionately allocated as follows: Cakravala (wall of the universe) 4, Himavanta 3, Great Ocean 2, Man's realm 1, total 10. If the 400 showers be then divided by this total of ten, the resulting quotient 40 should then be multiplied by the proportion allowed for each part of the middle world. So we get 160 showers for the Cakravala, 120 for Himavanta, 80 for the Great Ocean and only 40 for Man's domain. For a remainder 3 (Mars) there would be 300 showers; for 2 or 5 (Moon or Jupiter) 500 showers; for 4 or 6 (Mercury or Venus) 600 showers, with comparable proportional distribution.

To take as a concrete example the year April 1979–April 1980, that is Chula 1342, we find after subtracting 4 and then dividing by f7a remainder of 1, as shown above, which meant only 40 showers tor man's domain. Without wishing to advocate the reliability of his method, and I have carried out no control investigations for other years, I must recognize that this prognostication was remarkably accurate for the Chula year 1342, when the rains were insufficient and a shortage of water was experienced. Possibly the planetary deities wished to impress me with their powers on the occasion I happened to be in Bangkok examining the textual sources!

The Brahmans in their New Year prognostications included a forecast for the harvest of a more general nature, which might to some extent provide a hedge against the predictions based solely on rainfall.[5] In this case take the Chula year, multiply by 2, add 12 and then divide by 7. Predict according to the remainder: If it is 1 or 6 this is the most auspicious, indicating that 10 parts out of 11 of the seed grain will bear. Rice, meat and fruit will all be abundant, and everyone happy. Remainder 3 or 4 is considered of moderately good augury; half the seed grain will be lost, but people will be fairly well satisfied. In a year with a remainder 2 or 5 most of the seed grain will be destroyed by insects, and only 1 part out of 6 would be likely to bear; war and ruin could be expected. The worst, however, is indicated by a zero remainder, indicating that 10 parts out of 11 of the seed will be lost, with resultant famine, misery and ruin. Now for the Chula year 1342 (April 1979–April 1980) the calculation provided a remainder of 3.

If one waits a little longer, until the sixth month (May), when normally rain has begun to fall, there is a rough-and-ready means of prediction. According to the texts it is 'recommended by the learned of old', and is often accompanied by a graduated sketch of a cow.[6] According to this, much will depend on the height of the water on the first of the waxing of the sixth month, and it varies with the day the first happens to be:

If Sunday, level with cow's foot, very little water that year.
If Monday, level with cow's knee, little water that year.
If Tuesday, level with cow's belly, enough water to work fields.
If Wednesday, level with cow's sides, good water supply.
If Thursday, level with cow's chin, much water.
If Friday, level with cow's back, very much water.
If Saturday, level with cow's horns, too much, everywhere flooded.

A comment that may be made on some of the above methods is that not infrequently the fear of war is conjoined with the foretelling of a bad harvest. In earlier times whenever Siam's neighbours were suffering from the same unfavourable circumstances the dangers of marauding raids or more serious invasion had always to be feared.

After the considerable anxiety shown by the rural Thai in regard to prognostications for the essential rains one may be surprised to find that portents for the actual tilling are mainly limited to beginning every procedure on an auspicious day. This is partly because nature has generally been so kindly disposed to the Thai farmer that he has little to fear once enough water is assured. It is also partly because he is aware that at the capital an important ceremony will have been carried out which will ensure the productivity of the fields throughout the country. This is the First Ploughing which annually takes place in the sixth month, enjoying much popular support. I have described it in detail elsewhere, with mention of the particular dates which are auspicious for its performance, and the still eagerly watched omens drawn from the oxen's choice of commodity.[7] It is enough then for the Thai cultivator to bear in mind the auspicious days of the week on which to start each procedure.[8]

Sunday. This is a good day to start ploughing, at the beginning of the farming year; but not surprisingly it would be a most ill-omened day on which to sell padi, the end product.

Monday is the right day on which to begin sowing the seed rice. It is also a fortunate day, when the time comes, to cut the stakes to which the buffaloes will be tied when they are treading out the grain. The threshing floor should be levelled by collecting earth and placing it in the middle of the floor, before which one should face the *devatā* of the place and make an offering. It is an auspicious day on which to start threshing and also on which to put the grain in the granary.

Tuesday is the right day for making offerings to the rice spirit.

Wednesday is another good day for levelling the threshing floor or to start the buffaloes treading out the grain.

Thursday is the fortunate day for spreading the padi on the threshing floor, ready for treading out.

Friday is another good day to start ploughing, and also to make offerings to the rice spirit.

Saturday is both a good day on which to start ploughing, and an auspicious one on which to start reaping. It is another good day on which to cut the stakes to which the buffaloes will be tied.

On whichever auspicious day you start ploughing, you should first take nine leaf platters and pass them round, in accord with the Nāga's position, for just three circuits.[9] And on the Saturday on which you start reaping you should offer rice to the eight directions, placing the offering platters at the appropriate points on the field.

Until recent decades the trade of Siam was largely in the hands of foreigners, preponderantly Chinese, but the Thai now take an increasing part in the commerce and industry of their country. However the treatises always envisaged a certain proportion of the population as taking part in trade and, as compared with what we have seen in the case of agriculture, the amount of space given to the omens for profitable trading seems at first sight out of proportion. But then we must remember that trading, apart from the local 'floating market', involved travel, which was never wholly safe, any more than it is to-day as not a few bus travellers know to their cost. For a riverine people like the Thai, travel by water was traditional, and besides the main rivers a splendid network of canals served trade as well as irrigation. This is not to deny that a good deal of trade was carried out, before the advent of the motor roads, by bullock carts during the dry season using an almost equally extensive network of cart tracks.

Yet for year round travel, and almost essential during those months when the flood waters are out, many a rural family must depend very largely on the possession of good boats, even if they are not traders in rice, fish or fruits. The modern boats have lost their picturesque sails and sweeps, and have become dreadfully noisy. But so long as boats are built locally, can the following buyers' caveat be altogether ignored?[10]

If you buy a boat on *Sunday* the timber will not be well-joined. You may use it for a week but after that you will pay the penalty; so better sell it straight away. If you buy on *Monday* you will be fortunate and gain profit. A boat bought on *Tuesday* will destroy you; children will die and slaves flee. A boat bought on *Wednesday* would have timbers hollow and rotten; it should at once be got rid of. *Thursday's* boat will be most fortunate: well-shaped, with rat-breast knots, it will be excellent either for trade or for pleasure. If you buy on *Friday*, sorrows will disappear, you will be calm and happy, so don't hesitate. A boat bought on *Saturday* will be a grand one, with a knot on the seventh part, fit for nobles to go in procession and to receive rewards of clothes, silver and gold.

What means this reference to knots, notably one on the seventh part, apparently of portentous significance? Our treatise does not enlighten us, but it so happens that we have parallel evidence from a Burmese source which does. What the Thai text says is simply that a boat is considered to be divided into ten parts, each (in certain undisclosed circumstances) providing a prediction as follows:[11] 1. Will give much wealth. 2. A great prediction: will love everyone. 3. Plenty of rice and fish and lasting prosperity. 4. Maladies will molest. 5. Danger, even to death. 6. Excellent, will have many cattle and buffaloes under the house. 7. Will gain a wealthy handsome wife. 8. Poverty and ruin. 9. Much rice and fish. 10. A great prediction: will get the world's wealth.

Now according to Sangermano[12] a knot on one or other of ten divisions into which certain house timbers are divided provides omens closely corresponding to the above list. From this we may conclude that a knot in any one of the ten parts would be the mark denoting that particular omen. Thus one in the seventh division, as mentioned for Saturday, would, at least in one respect, be a very favourable portent.

In setting out on any journey the movements of animals should be noted and care taken not to face the Śeṣa Nāga (world serpent). For Sunday travel it is important to have washed the face first.

For Monday one should have slept well; for Tuesday eaten something sweet; for Wednesday eaten rice; for Thursday one should have anointed the face with stove ashes; for Friday one should make a stop on the way; and for Saturday one should only start when calm in mind. Certain watches (1 on Sunday, 2 on Monday, 3 on Tuesday) are to be avoided as then Kāla (Yama) stalks abroad; while travel on Saturday at nightfall means death to the traveller and his servants.[13]

Aside from such practicalities one cannot complain of not being warned by means of omens of the likely outcome of any trading venture by boat, embarked upon on any particular day of the lunar month. This information is communicated to us by the Devacara, or Travelling (Walking) *Devatā*, or rather by his exact position in the boat or ship on the day we have in mind. He indicates by his presence, rather than causes (for the outlook may be good or bad), the fate which awaits the voyager on that day. As this information was communicated at some remote time to the seers, to make use of it we have to refer to the appropriate treatise.[14]

The vessel, of whatever size, is conceived as being divided into six vertical parts, in any one of which the Devacara can manifest. These are the ship's bottom, the hold, the stern, the sides, the rigging, the top of the mast. In every month the Devacara locates:

(1) In the ship's bottom on the 9th and 10th waxing, and 2nd, 4th, 12th and 13th waning. To sail would be fatal and the ship lost.

(2) In the hold on the 1st, 6th, 7th and 8th waxing and the 5th waning. The omen is bad, for the ship will tremble and may strike rocks.

(3) In the stern, on the 3rd waning. A bad presage because an enemy plans evil.

(4) In the sides on the 2nd, 3rd, and 11th waxing and the 1st, 6th, 10th and 11th waning. These are the best days and portend profitable trading voyages. An exception is made for the 12th waxing, when navigation will be difficult.

(5) In the rigging, on the 4th, 13th and 15th waxing, when the omen is favourable; but on the 9th waning it is unfavourable.

(6) On the top of the mast, on the 5th and 14th waxing, and on

the 8th waning. There will be danger from strong winds, with the likely loss of the vessel.

The 14th and 15th waning are also said to be profitable, but our text omits to state where on those days the Devacara is situated.

Rāma's progress

The treatise strongly advises this system to be considered most carefully before setting out to trade.[15] It provides the omens, favourable or otherwise, for setting forth at each daytime watch, on each of the seven days.[16] Since time is of the essence, the system may be considered as remotely astrological, and in looking through the list I have noticed that watches 1, 7 and 3 are seldom good, 2 and 5 never bad, while 4 and 6 may be either. But what gives the system its chief interest is the reinforcing the efficacy of such purely calendrical data by linking each time with some well-known event, fortunate or not, in the *Rāmakien*. However the supply of such suitable occurrences, as known to the compilers, who may have been Thai, soon runs out. So we are left with a number of exploits of the planetary deities, rivalling those of the Greek gods, and the mythological origins of which, though sometimes obvious, in others might be difficult to trace.

A selection of typical predictions will suffice for our purpose. These I take from the printed text, and it would not be surprising if the manuscripts show considerable variation in detail. In the examples I now give, the day is followed by the watch number.

Sunday, 1. If you start you will wear yourself out, as Rāma did when, following the stag, he lost Sīdā and had much trouble.

Sunday, 3. You must not start for this was when Lak (Lakṣman) was pierced by Kumbhakarna's Mohasak spear.

Sunday, 6. Go east and you will make profit, as did Rāma when he ascended the throne.

Sunday, 7. This was when Rāma killed the *yakṣas* Tut (Dūshana) and Korn (Khara); so go now and you will succeed.

Monday, 2. Go west to succeed, for it was when Pipek (Vibhiṣana) was victorious.

Monday, 3. If you go you will be ill and die, for it was when Thonphi lost to Pālī.

Monday, 6. If you travel east you will profit, for it was when Pipek was rewarded.

Tuesday, 3. If you go there will be trouble, for it was when Rāma used Lak to fetch Sīdā.

Tuesday, 7. If you go you will be ill, for it was when Pipek was defeated by his people.

Saturday, 5. Go north and you will gain wealth. It was when Sīdā gained happiness.

It is more especially during the latter part of the week that a dearth of suitable *Rāmakien* incidents is experienced, and so we find increasingly this sort of thing:

Monday, 1. If you go you will lose, for it was when the Sun met Rāhu.

Tuesday, 6. If you go you will die, for it was when Śiva wagered and lost the world.

Thursday, 5. Go north and you will gain wealth. It was when Venus went to study all the arts.

Thursday, 3. If you go north you will lose your goods to an enemy. It was when Mars committed adultery and was caught.

Thursday, 4. Go, you will gain wealth on the road. It was when Venus followed the Sun and was rewarded.

Thursday, 7. If you go an enemy will cause you loss. It was when Mars committed adultery with the Moon. His relative, Jupiter, caught him.

Friday, 7. Don't go. It was when a certain king went to capture a city, but failed. He returned empty-handed.

Saturday, 1. If you go you will be wounded. It was when the Sun went to store some goods, and he met a bandit.

Saturday, 7. If you go you will lose goods and get into trouble. It was when the Sun sent Saturn to catch Mars and he caught him.[17]

Finally we come to a system of much grander conception, in which the planetary deities show less human characteristics. Indeed they are accorded full cosmic powers, acting together with the great gods of Hinduism. This I will call

The Descent of the Devas[18]

The basic supposition is that each day of the lunar month, both waxing and waning, one or two planetary deities descend into our atmosphere, accompanied by one or sometimes two of the great Hindu gods, and also the Devacara (Walking *Devatā*). The last-mentioned each day enters one or other part of the human body, and would thus originally have apprised us of the nature of the omen to be expected that day. Now that we are no longer sensitive to such communications we have to consult the books in which what we need to know has been placed on record by the wise men of old. The nature of the omen is partly decided, in astrological manner, by the benefic or malefic character of the planets concerned, but more important, for better or for worse, is the nature of the great Hindu deity, be he Indra, Viṣṇu, Śiva or Yama.

It would appear that the power of the omen for each day comes into effect at 6 a.m. and tends to wear off at noon. The justification for my considering this system here is that it gives pride of place to the omens for trading, and it is noteworthy that a day that is unlucky for water may be the reverse for travel by land, and vice versa. However I think the great interest is the comprehensiveness of the portents, covering many of the more domestic activities to which we have already alluded. Indeed for the average person, not much concerned with affairs of state, this system provides all-embracing divine guidance. To obtain the evidence on which to base some conclusions one must consider all the days, both waxing and waning, but it will not be necessary to repeat all the details. To begin with the *waxing:*

1st. Mercury, Jupiter and Viṣṇu all three come down and give the most auspicious omens, Devacara being in the mind. The nobles will provide wealth, and trading by boat will be most successful, because of a widow. However you should not travel by land. If you propose marriage, good, you will live long together. If today you buy slaves, oxen or buffaloes, cut or sew cloth or don new clothes, such actions will all be very fortunate. Moreover a darkish person with staring eyes will bring you wealth. However it would be advisable not to visit any officials today, as you may lose some cattle and poultry.

2nd. Mars is everywhere and Mercury comes down into the atmosphere. They are of bad portent, and this is accentuated by the descent also of Yama (Death). Devacara is in the feet. Don't attempt anything auspicious,[19] don't trade today, don't build a house or propose marriage. You would quarrel and die apart.

3rd. Moon falls in all the forest, and Mars, Candakumara and Yama descend and give bad omen. Devacara is in the chin. Don't do auspicious things...however trade with the nobles will be profitable.

4th. Sun falls on all the land, Moon and Mercury descend into the atmosphere, and this presages well. Devacara is in the leg. Quickly do auspicious things, but avoid trading today. However you will gain by going to see the nobles today.

5th. Kāla (=Yama) descends in the water everywhere, and Sun descends in the atmosphere, this being of bad omen. Devacara is in the feet. Don't do auspicious things. However if you trade by land you will profit, but travel by boat would lead to loss.

6th. Ketu falls on all the land, and Venus and Śiva descend into the atmosphere, giving the omen. Devacara is in the forehead. If you trade by water you will make a profit, but don't go by land as then you will lose. Don't buy oxen etc. etc.

7th. Rāhu is in the water and Sun descends in the air, also Yama, giving bad omen. Devacara is in the ears. Don't do auspicious things, as illness will follow. Don't trade by land as you will lose money, male and female slaves. But if you trade by boat that will be profitable, especially if you deal with the nobles. Don't propose marriage.

8th. Saturn descends on the mountain. Sun and Mṛitayu (=Yama) descend into the air, giving bad omen. Devacara is in the sides Don't do auspicious things...don't buy slaves or cattle, you'll lose money.

9th. Venus and Jupiter descend, while Śiva gives the omen. Devacara is in the eyes. Quickly do auspicious things...you will profit if you trade, either by land or water, but don't go too far afield...

10th. Jupiter, Saturn and Yama descend. The omen is bad. Devacara is in the head. Don't travel by boat, you will lose animals, but land trading with the nobles will be profitable. Don't propose...

11th. Mercury and Kāla descend, but so also does Viṣṇu who gives a good omen. Devacara is in the stomach. Quickly do auspicious things...but don't travel by land for you would be ill and die. However boat trading will be profitable...

12th. Mars descends into the hearts of the great. Mercury and Yama also, giving a bad omen. Devacara is in the head. Don't do auspicious things...fire will burn the house. Don't trade by land or water, etc.

13th. Moon descends in the air, as also does Viṣṇukarma, giving the omen. Devacara is in the chin. Quickly do auspicious things...but don't trade by land or water, or you will be ill. And don't buy animals...

14th. Sun, Saturn and Kāla descend, giving bad omen. Devacara is in the shoulder. Don't do auspicious things...Don't buy animals and don't travel by land or water, etc.

15th. Kāla falls in every village, and Sun also descends in the air. But Viṣṇu also descends so that the presage is good. Devacara is in the back. Quickly do auspicious things, but don't trade by land or water as you would lose. And don't go into the jungle for you would be taken ill.

Now the *waning:*

1st. Ketu falls everywhere, Venus also descends into the air, and so does Śiva, giving the omen. Devacara is in the feet. Quickly do auspicious things...If you trade by land or water you will do well, from a fair man.

2nd. Rāhu falls in the fields and Mṛitayu descends, giving the omen. Devacara is in the hands. Don't do auspicious things... don't trade by water or land, you'll lose. Don't buy animals... but if you visit the nobles you will profit.

3rd. Saturn falls in all the streams. Mercury descends in the air, and so does Yama, giving bad portent. Devacara is in the feet. Don't do auspicious things...Go anywhere except the jungle and trade by land or water will be successful. Don't buy oxen or visit the nobles.

4th. Venus alights in the chief centre. Jupiter and Indra descend, giving the omen. Devacara is in the teeth. Quickly do auspicious things, except proposing marriage or putting rice in the granary. Trade by water or land will be profitable.

5th. Jupiter falls in the jungle and Moon descends in the atmosphere, while Yama also descends, giving bad omen. Devacara is in the chin. Don't do auspicious things...If you trade by water or land, you will get profit from the nobles; but don't go to the north as you would lose animals. You can get wealth from the forest.

6th. Mercury falls in an auspicious place, while Mars and Viṣṇu descend and give the omen. Devacara is in the forehead. Quickly do auspicious things...Trade by land or water will be profitable, also buying animals...

7th. Mars falls in the water, and Yama descends giving bad omen. Devacara is in the back. Don't do auspicious things... Trade by land or water will be profitable, and visiting the nobles good...

8th. Moon falls everywhere and Candakumara descends giving bad omen. Devacara is in the face. Don't do auspicious things... don't go far afield as you will lose animals...but trade by land or water to the nobles will be profitable.

9th. Sun falls in the gardens of good people everywhere, and Venus and Viṣṇukarma descend giving good omen. Devacara is in the head. Quickly do auspicious things. Trading by land or water will be good...but keep away from the lords or you will lose goods...

10th. Kāla falls on all the land, and Saturn descends in the air, as also does Phra Sulī (a demon chief), giving bad omen. Don't do auspicious things...Don't trade by water but by land only and you will gain profit. If you visit the nobles you should obtain wealth.

11th. Ketu falls on all the land. Venus and Indra also descend, giving the omen. Devacara is in the feet. Trade by land or water will result in profit, from a woman buyer. Don't litigate, you'll lose money...

12th. Rāhu falls to the earth, and Yama and Indra descend in the air, giving bad omen. Devacara is in the soles of the feet. Don't do auspicious things...Don't trade by water as you would lose animals, but by land trading will be profitable.

13th. Saturn falls in the house of the women Brahmans, and Moon and Mercury descend in the atmosphere. Devacara is in the ears. Quickly do auspicious things...trading by land or water, as also visiting the nobles. But don't go into the jungle...

14th. Venus falls on all the threshing floors, Jupiter descends in the air, while Indra gives the omen. Devacara is in the crown of the head. Quickly do auspicious things...but don't put padi on the threshing floor, or in the granary. Don't borrow things...or litigate...

15th. Jupiter falls in a central place, while Viṣṇu and Indra descend, giving the omen. Devacara is in the mind. Quickly do auspicious things...but don't go in the jungle. Don't trade or litigate...

Contradictions in the details would be more apparent had I given them more fully, and might have tended to obscure the main trends. And my persistent mention of the Devacara's location is intended to provide material that may help towards elucidating the problem of this deity's nature. One may first note that the omens are good in both waxing and waning days 1, 4, 6, 9, 11, 13, 15, the only difference being that 14 is bad in the waxing and good in the waning. This agreement results usually from the controlling major Hindu deity being the same (or similarly minded) on all the corresponding days of waxing and waning. Looking at the waxing days we find that the first starts with Mercury (Wednesday) and the starter in each subsequent day continues backwards through the days of the week, until it repeats Sunday and then includes Rāhu and Ketu, before starting the series again back from Saturn. With the waning days the 1st starts with Ketu and proceeds accordingly each day, but, as already stated, the nature of the omen is usually decided by the major Hindu deity manifesting that day. An Indian origin for the system is indicated by the mention of female Brahmans on the 13th waning—in addition to the importance accorded to the Hindu deities.

A surprising feature which particularly concerns us here is that waxing days are not considered the most suitable for trading ventures, and those days recommended are not necessarily of good omen generally. Herein of course lies another point of apparent contradiction. Thus waxing days 1, 6, 7, 11 are accounted fortunate for boat-trading only, 5 and 10 for land trading only, and 3 and

9 for both methods. The rest are evidently considered unlucky. Of the waning, on the contrary, 1, 3, 4, 5, 6, 7, 8, 9, 11, and 13 are lucky for *both* means of trading, 10 and 12 for land travel only, while only 2, 14 and 15 are ruled out.

Some indications for travellers are included in the third part of the Thai-Cambodian manuscript later to be considered (p. 138). Thus clouds with the appearance of a peacock or a flying fox are auspicious. That applies also to a bird of prey if seen on the left, but if on the right it is unlucky (75). A cloud like a *nāga's* tail is lucky for the traveller (78e), while a deformed black-edged crescent moon portends peaceful conditions for traders by land (82b). A cloud looking like a cow presages a peaceful journey for the the traveller, but one like a bull indicates a brawl ahead (74 d, e). Peace and good health are foretold for the traveller by five clouds, alternately blue and white, with above them four rose-petal-like clouds (76 e).

NOTES TO CHAPTER VII

1. *B* I, pp. 117f. In a critique, in Thai, of the New Year Festival (*Praḥbenī noäng näi deśakal*, Bangkok, 1963. p. 45) Phya Anuman seeks to justify the old belief on the grounds that it is not for man to presume to judge how the *nāgas* should act, their wonders to perform.
2. *B* I, pp. 119 ff.
3. *B* I, p. 115. A. Leclère, *Cambodge, Fêtes Civiles et Religieuses*, Paris, 1916, p. 79, note (1) records the official Cambodian prognostications by the same method for the year 1904.
4. For such calculations the Chulasakaraj (Civil Era) beginning A.D. 638 is always used.
5. *B* I, p. 116.
6. *B* III, p. 76.
7. *Siamese State Ceremonies*, London, 1931, Ch. XXI, and *Supplementary Notes*, London 1971, p. 29.
8. *B* I, p. 110.
9. See p. 77, in regard to the position of the Śeṣa Nāga.
10. *B* I, p. 107.
11. ibid.
12. op.cit., p. 143.
13. *B* II, p. 80.
14. *B* II, pp. 108 f. At least one MS. in the National Library, Bangkok, shows a diagram of a junk indicating the various positions of the Devacara.
15. *B* I, pp. 72–76.
16. For divination purposes a watch of $1\frac{1}{2}$ hours duration is used, since the usual watch of 3 hours would be too vague. From 6 a.m. there are eight day watches of $1\frac{1}{2}$ hours each. The tabulation begins always with the watch of the same number as the day, e.g. Wednesday, watch 4.
17. Night travel was evidently not envisaged in earlier times and prescriptions for such found in our text (*B* II, pp. 77–79) must be seen as 19th century additions. They give no omens but only associate each night watch with an incident in literature. These are drawn not only from the Jātakas and *Rāmakien*, but also from the stories *Phra Rot* and *Phra Lo*, 18th–19th Century Thai compositions.
18. *B* I, pp. 78–88. Bastian, op.cit., p. 429 evidently had access through a translator to a MS. treatise of the Descent of the Devata, but he omitted the portents, and what he says about the *devatā* is enough to show that his source differed largely from mine. He also confuses Devacara with a similarly pronounced Thai word meaning 'pulse'.
19. By anything 'auspicious' (*maṅgala*) is meant any activity or ritual such as proposing marriage or house-building which, while optimistically fortunate, could be the reverse if carried out on a day of ill-omen.

CHAPTER VIII

LOST, STOLEN OR STRAYED.

Profits accumulated from crops planted and harvested on tradiționally the right days and from trading ventures which duly respected the admonitions of the soothsayers, have no doubt at teast contributed to the prosperity and sense of well-being of a great many Thai families over the centuries. And as everywhere else this side of paradise such success, even to the relative degree to be expected at village level, has always awakened the envy of the less fortunate, leading only too frequently to theft.

In the larger households the question that immediately arises is whether the thief is not just as likely to be a servant or some disgruntled relative, as a robber from without. And then a valuable object could have been just lost, cattle could have just strayed, although there was every reason to fear the worst. In any case, in which direction to begin a search was surely a matter for skilled divination.

In the predictions it will be seen that the importance of obtaining news, as a preliminary to recovery of the vanished possessions, looms large. So I must say something of the system of apprehending wrongdoers which prevailed prior to the establishment of modern policing in the present century. And since, as any Thai newspaper reader will know, this is not always as effective as it might be, there is much to be said for the old community spirit surviving in the more rural areas.

According to the old-time law everyone living within five *sen* (one eighth of a mile) of the place where a crime was committed had to take up the search. Anyone successful in catching the robber was rewarded with a third of the value of the property stolen, the rest being refunded to the victim, but failure was punished with a fine to be used as compensation. However a portion of the compensation went to the local government because the victim of the robbery had not taken sufficient care. Naturally the system was reinforced by spying, everyone being expected to inform on his neighbour, while heavy punishment was the lot of anyone who failed to report if he knew of any person planning to steal or pillage.

The horary method

It is interesting to find that the method advocated by the Thai treatises for finding thieves and lost or strayed possessions is derived from the Indian system of horary or Prasna astrology. This is not in any way concerned with the horoscope of the individual who has sustained the loss. It depends on the horoscope of the time questions are put to the astrologer as to what steps should be taken. The Prasna system was noticed by Dubois in eighteenth century Hindu India when he wrote that 'it is possible to find out, not only the place where a stolen article is secreted, but also the sex and caste of the thief. They are also able to ascertain whether or not the stolen article will be recovered, according as the sign, the planet, and the star which correspond to the time at which the consultation takes place are favourable or the reverse.'[1]

Things do not seem to have changed very much in this respect in modern India. B.V.Raman, who has recently given us an English translation of the Sanskrit *Prasna Tantra*, as compiled in the sixteenth century A. D., states in his introduction that 'in my practice most of the predictions made by me essentially based on this book have been remarkably fulfilled.' And, as he stresses, the important characteristic of horary astrology is that the time of a query is known exactly and in this time 'lie embedded seeds of the result.'[2] In other words the question is prompted by the cosmic conditions generating the situation.

I shall now quote a few stanzas from Raman's translation which will serve to illustrate the similarities as well as the differences when we come to the Thai treatise. We need not trouble, any more than do the Thai, about the astrological technicalities, except to mention that nowadays these are obtained merely from consulting the modern astronomical ephemerides. And I shall omit them after the first two examples.

Stanza 76: If the lord of the 5th house is in the ascendant or the Moon is in the ascendant, aspected by the lord of the 4th, the lost money is to be found in the expected place. Stanza 78: When Mars is in the 7th or 8th, the wealth will not be secured by the querent as it will be in the protection of another person. If Rāhu is in the ascendant and the Sun is in the 8th, the wealth or property will not be secured. The wealth can be secured if either the Moon or Jupiter becomes the lord of the 7th, 8th, 4th or 10th. Stanza 80: When... the thief will return the wealth. When... the lost wealth will not be recovered. Stanza 81: The thief will himself steal the property and run away to his abode when... The thief will be caught with the stolen property if... Stanza 82: The thief is in the place of the theft if... He will have bolted away from the place if... If...the thief will have left the town limits. Stanza 86: If... the lost property will respectively be hidden near the door, or inside the premises, or in the backyard of the house. Stanza 87: If the question refers to money inadvertently lost, say that it is in the place dropped, if... Stanza 88: If 'in what direction is the lost property to be secured' is the question, say that it is in the east, south, west or north according as the ... Stanza 92: If... the thief will be caught. If... the thief will be apprehended along with the property. Stanza 98: If the query is 'who is the thief?', say he is a member of the household of the querent if... If... say the thief lives near the querent's house. Stanza 99: If... the thief is one belonging to the same household. If...the thief is the querent's own servant. Stanza 106: According as ... the thief will respectively be a youth, a boy, a middle-aged man, a young person, an old man or a very old person.

However little one may know of astrology one will readily appreciate that all such predictions as the above are dependent on knowing the relations of the planets, benefic or malefic, to the signs that they occupy at that particular time, not merely on the time as such. The absence of such information robs the predictions of all pretence of 'scientific accuracy' such as the original Prasna system claims. For the Thai, with the bliss of ignorance, all months and days are the same, and one only needs to know the watch (of $1\frac{1}{2}$ hours as used for divination purposes). From our point of view, however, the compensation is the graphic picture of local hopes and fears which the naturalized Thai system affords.

According to this, the soothsayer can take either the watch when the inquirer comes to ask his questions, or the watch in which the property disappeared.[3] Such is the power of the seven numbers that there would be no special answer for the eight watch; it would be a repetition of that prescribed for the first.

LOST, STOLEN OR STRAYED

Watch 1. A darkish man stole the goods. If they have been found someone with a sore on his forehead will bring the news. They are north of the house, not far from the owner. They will be returned in five days, but failing that will never be returned. If slaves have fled, oxen or buffaloes strayed, look for them to the N.E. or S.

Watch 2. Property has been lost. Say that a corpulent woman of middling height with long arms and with a sore below the mouth will tell you that someone living in the house stole the goods and gave them to someone else who took them away. If silver and gold are stolen by a woman they will be recovered. If stolen by a servant they are hidden in a clothes chest; on searching, they can be got back. If it's cattle that have been stolen they will probably not be recovered. They've been taken to the west, and after four days cannot be retrieved. If a boat has been stolen it has been taken to the water. If one looks to the S.E. it will be found in four days. If gold is lost it has gone west. If swords and spears are lost they are hidden under the head of a sleeping mat. They may be found up to seven days search, but not later.

Watch 3. A fair man with curly hair, a wound and white spots on his back and his head damaged, has taken the stolen property to the west. In seven days you may expect news and in eight should get the property back, but after that no hope. If it's gold, silver and clothes, you should get news in three days and the goods may be found up to one month. If it's money and knives that have been stolen, the thief could not take them away, so he dropped them in water. Gold and silver you should get back. If oxen have strayed, look to the S.W., buffaloes to the N.E., and elephants the S.W. near the water's edge, where however they may be dead.

Watch 4. Say that a dark woman with a sore on the breast and another on the left of the mouth, entered the house, stole the goods and went S.W. or N. If it was gold it can be got back by looking to the N.E., but not after seven days. Looking for silver may end in a dispute. If it's elephants that have strayed with their hobbles broken, go to the south and you'll get them back; but if it's oxen go quickly to the south and look near a canal. If a boat has been lost look for it to the west. Silver and gold would have been hidden near a canal distant from the house 1 *wa* (6ft. 6in.) to 1 *sen* (44 yards). Someone has taken the boat to one landing place for seven days, and to another for five days, after which time it cannot be found. If spears and swords have been stolen they have been hidden under a mat, and of this a woman will bring the news. But if she brings bad news that is more likely to be true.

Watch 5. Say that a darkish man with a sore on neck, breast, jaw or side, took the goods to the north, where he has hidden them at a white ants' hill near a big tree; or he has sunk them in water. After ten days you will have news and will get them back. It it is gold or silver a person living in the house is the thief. If cattle or poultry have been stolen, they've been taken to the south-east and in eight days they will be returned, after a darkish man has brought the news. If elephants, oxen or buffaloes are lost, look to the north and west. You will get them in two days or, if not, in four days you will have news. But if swords and spears have gone they will not be retrieved.

Watch 6. The lost property was stolen by a corpulent man of the lower class with a sore on his forehead, living to the west. He took the things to the east, and confided them to a child in a distant place. You'll get news, but from two men having different opinions. If it's cattle or poultry that are lost, they'll be brought back. If they were taken to the north, someone will bring news and you will have them back in nine days. If now you should happen to have fever, it is caused by the house spirit, so make offerings to him and in nine days you will be cured. If elephants, oxen and buffaloes are lost, go and look to the east, and in two days you will find them in the fields. If silver and gold have been taken they are hidden at the head of a bed; someone will bring news and you will get them back. The stolen boat has been taken to the north.

Watch 7. Say that the property was taken south-east by a thin man with curly hair and a wound on the knee. He took it to a big tree. In three days you should have news, and in four days get it back, but not after that. If poultry or cattle have been stolen, say they cannot be got back, and they have gone to the north-west. If money has been stolen it was by a darkish woman who gave it to a man. You will get it back in ten days. If you are taken ill, make offerings to the N.W., and you will be cured. If elephants have strayed look to the N.E., near the river bank and you will get them back. But if a female elephant has been stolen they've taken it to sell in a town. Look to the N.W. and in ten days you should get it back, but not after that. If oxen and buffaloes have strayed, they've gone to the N.W. Someone will come with news and they will be brought back. But if it is a cow buffalo you will not get it back. If a boat is lost, it is to the N.W. Offer a reward and you will get it back, only much damaged.

The Three Eye Watches[4]

Other methods of tracing lost property range from a simple casting of lots to a development of the watch system which allows rather more refinement in the predictions without of course approaching that of astrology. This it does by taking account not only of the watch, but also of the particular day or night of the week and whether the moon is waxing or waning. I cannot say whether this development took place locally or elsewhere.

As we have seen, for divination the day has eight watches of $1\frac{1}{2}$ hours each, starting from 6 a.m. and the night has eight similar watches starting from 6 p.m. According to the Three Eye Watch system each watch of day or night is given a Pāli name which from one to seven is a slightly modified version of the planets' names. However we can ignore these names and just think of the planets by their week-day numbers, except that as no eighth planet is here recognized the eighth watch whether of day or night is a repetition of the first. That is straightforward enough, but a complication now arises in that the daytime watches, instead of following the order of the days, are arranged 1, 6, 4, 2, 7, 5, 3, 1, while the night watches are arranged 1, 5, 2, 6, 3, 7, 4, 1.

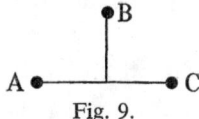

Fig. 9.

Now we look at Fig. 9 showing the Three Eye Watches, A, B, C. If the querent puts his question on a waxing moon day you start to count from eye A and turn to eye B; if on a waning moon day you start from eye B, and proceed to eye C. Supposing that he comes on a Monday, waxing moon, day watch 1, you start to count from eye A which will be 2 because Monday is day 2. Then you proceed via eye B through the watches which after 2 are 7, 5, 3, 1. And 1 being the watch concerned falls to eye B. So you foretell according to the omens prescribed for eye B. Or take the case of an inquirer who presents himself on a Friday of the waning, night watch 2. As it is waning you must count from eye B, and as Friday is day 6 and watch 3 comes next to 6 in the above order, you reach eye C and foretell the omens accordingly. All this presents a little difficulty for quick calculation and the treatise suggests means of ready reckoning on the fingers.

Will the goods be found or not? A. Cannot be found. B. With difficulty. C. Quickly.

What kind of person is the thief? A. An ex-monk who lives in the house, has taken it to somewhere near the river bank. B. A woman is the thief and she took the things to a place where there is a bush near the house; or she hid it in the roots of a big tree near the well and covered it with a heavy object. C. A big dark man took the things and he hid them near a big tree, covering them with a heavy object.

Is the thief dark or fair? A. A dark person living in the same house. B. A fair woman living in the house stole the things, or it may have been an ex-monk. C. A dark person from outside the house is the thief.

Will some lost poultry and cattle be found? A. Will soon be recovered. B. May or may not be found, equally likely. C. Cannot be got back.

In what direction have the stolen goods been taken? A. Look to the north-east and north. It will be difficult to find them, but someone will bring news. Or they will be by a big tree. B. Look to the S.W. and S. A relative may have taken them. C. A stranger has taken them. He lives to the west. A neighbour will show you the way, it is not very far and not very near.

In some cases an answer only seems to be forthcoming from one particular Eye. Thus:

Will agricultural implements, knives, hoes, spades etc. be found? A. They will have gone altogether if not recovered that day.

LOST, STOLEN OR STRAYED

Will the buffaloes that have been taken from their wallows be recovered? C. Yes, if found in three days, to the north, about three 'calls' away.

Has the thief spent the money yet? A scarcely reassuring prediction comes from all three Eyes: He is just now at the gaming place.

It may be added that as with the *Prasna Tantra* our Thai treatise is not absolutely confined to the search for lost property. So we have:

Will the baby be born easily or difficultly? A. Easily. B. After a long time. C. With much trouble. Or even less optimistically: A. Not for a long time. B. With difficulty, a long time ahead. C. With great difficulty.

When will the baby be born? A. At dawn, easily. B. Noon or evening. C. At night.

A boy or a girl? A. Boy. B. Girl. C. Boy.

When will the expected person return? A. To-day. B. Still detained by business and will not come for two days. C. Will return in three days.

What is the prognosis for the sick person? A. Will recover slowly, it is not serious. B. Will have trouble, but will finally recover. C. Two to one will die.

When will the sick person recover? A. In two days. C. Will be ill for three days and then will be surprised at getting well.

Other methods

For the inquirer as to the return of an absent person, this alternative is available, the portents manifesting through the behaviour of the querent.

Behaviour	Portent
Sits holding an ear.	Not yet returning.
Sits touching feet.	Will return in four days.
Sits touching forehead or back.	Will come presently.
Asking if arrested person will be released, sits touching stomach, chin or mouth.	Has been released.

Sits down only 1 cubit away.   Is dead.
Sits 2 cubits away.   Is very ill.
Sits 3 cubits away.   Is dead.
Sits 4 cubits away.   Is ill, but not seriously.

For the querent wishing to know whether a sick person will recover, the remainders method offers a 'second opinion', not necessarily any more reassuring. Take the patient's age, less one year, multiply by 18 and then divide by 7. Remainder 3, 7 (sic) or 0, will certainly die; 1, 2, 4 will not die and will soon recover; 5 or 6, will not die, it is not serious. Or take the age similarly, multiply by 9, divide by 7. Remainder 7 or 0 very serious, will die; 1, 2, 3, will not die, if well nursed; 4, serious, difficult to cure.[5]

Ordeals

Reverting to the subject of stolen possessions, it not unnaturally often happened that in large households suspicion fell on a number of persons without sufficient evidence to commit any one of them. It was then often the practice both in Siam and in Burma to round up the servants and call in a reputable soothsayer who would proceed to hand each of them a portion of the stem of Convolvulus (*Ipomoea reputans*), all of the same length. At the same time he warns them to keep the stems carefully as, if in the possession of a thief, the stem of this plant has the property of growing longer. Next day he returns to examine the stems and—most probably—finds that the thief has cut off a portion of his stem as a precautionary measure. Today this divination might hardly be expected to work, if only because one had not enough servants to try it on, nor did it always work in the old days, depending as it did on the psychological skill of the soothsayer.

This example of private trial by ordeal naturally brings us to the larger question of public trial by ordeal. It is a subject which from its spectacular nature drew the attention of most of the early writers on Siam. But an accurate and comprehensive study, with translations of the law texts concerned, had to await the scholarship of the late Colonel G. E. Gerini, whose publication is unfortunately not everywhere accessible.[6] It is on his study that I base the short account given here, for trial by ordeal cannot be overlooked in any work on divination.

In Siam this form of trial was firmly based on ancient Indian precepts and was mainly by fire or by water, the two great purifying agents of the Hindus. Such trial was called for in both criminal and civil cases where the evidence of witnesses was deemed unsatisfactory. In the case of litigants the Siamese law was more equitable than the Indian in that both were required to undergo the ordeal, thus preventing the bringing of false charges.

The Ordeal by Diving was the most usual in Siam (and also in neighbouring countries), but it was not revived after the fall of Ayudhyā. However the necessary pits were dug near the lawcourts in Bangkok, and were not filled in until about a century after the foundation of this new capital. There also was set up the altar of Kāla (Death), on the site prepared for Ordeals by Fire. For the Diving Ordeal two stakes were driven into the bottom of the pond, ten feet apart. Arrayed in white, a cangue collar round their necks and safety rope round their waists, the competitors, after invoking Kāla and the water deities, entered the water up to their necks. Holding their respective stakes, a pole was placed across the shoulders of both, on which an official pressed at the signal from a gong. He who remained under longer was the victor.

With a people so impatient for knowledge of the future as are the Thai, it is not surprising that prior to entering the water the contestants were allowed to have a preliminary game of cockfighting, which would provide prognostics for the major undertaking. There was also much betting amongst the bystanders, who were also frequently provided with a good deal of amusement. Moreover it may still be that some of the old mechanical representations, formerly so much in demand, can still be found in working order at some temple festival. The scene represented was that of a Court of Justice, with two litigants engaged in diving. Much was the merriment caused when one of the divers emerges to find his opponent still below water, and he hastens to dive down again in the hope of escaping detection.

According to La Loubère, writing late in the seventeenth century, in Siam 'Everyone practises from his youth to familiarize himself with fire, and to continue a long time under water.'[7] Which brings us to say something about the Ordeal by Fire. Of course everyone was then acquainted, as everyone still is, with the touching incident in the *Rāmakien* when Sīdā triumphantly underwent the ordeal. In Siam anyone undergoing the ordeal had to prepare by fasts and offerings to Kāla, to prevent the latter's minions from carrying him off during the proceedings. He was also purified by ablutions and protected from adverse influences by a diadem and, round the wrists, threads of unspun cotton. During the test the judges sat under an awning feasting at the expense of the competitors. The fire over which both accuser and accused must walk with bare feet, when the gong sounded, was of a ten-inch layer of live coals in a ditch ten feet long, while officials pressed heavily on their shoulders. Perhaps this pressure largely stifled the fire's action. To quote La Loubère again 'as the Siamese are accustomed to go with naked feet and have the sole of the foot hard like horn, they say that it is very common that the fire spares them, provided they rest the foot upon the coals; for the way to burn themselves is to go quickly and lightly.'[8]

In criminal cases execution was of course liable to follow the exercise provided by either type of ordeal. Possibly the last and most memorable occasion in which a large-scale Ordeal by Water was followed by such a sequel is that ordained by King Tak after he had defeated in 1770 the army of a rebellious high priest at Müang Fang.[9] The captured monks were assembled and those that confessed were unfrocked and set free. But many continued to maintain their innocence and were required to undergo a water-ordeal to prove it. The king had a shrine erected where the offerings were made to the *devas* who were adjured to cause all who had infringed the rule of the Order to be defeated in the trial. The king then sat down on a chair by the river-bank to watch. Many of the monks succeeded, but others did not. They were then divested of their robes and executed. It is recorded that after their cremation the ashes were mixed with lime and lacquer and used to whitewash the *stūpa* containing sacred relics at Müang Fang.

NOTES TO CHAPTER VIII

1. Dubois, op.cit., p. 387.
2. B.V.Raman, *Prasna Tantra*, (Horary Astrology), 3rd edn. Bangalore, 1975.
3. *B* II, pp. 65–68.
4. *B* II, pp. 60–65; also *BSMB*. pp. 493 ff.
5. *BSMB*, p. 476. Portents from the querent's behaviour are reminiscent of Varāhamihira Ch. LI.
6. G.E.Gerini, 'Trial by Ordeal in Siam and the Siamese Law of Ordeals', *Imp. and Asiatic Qly. Rev.* Jan-April, 1895, pp. 415–424, July 1895,. pp. 156–175.
7. De la Loubère, *A New Historical Relation of the Kingdom of Siam*, London, 1693, p. 87.
8. ibid., p. 86.
9. *Annals of Ayudhyā* (Royal Sign Manual Edition), in Thai, Bangkok, 1913, Vol. III., p. 50.

CHAPTER IX

DREAMS

Dreams have been universally regarded as portentous, and their interest is that they shed a revealing light on the psychology of any particular people from a rather different angle than any otherwise available. Generally speaking they follow the same rules of symbolism as is found with the omens actually observed in waking hours, though the association of ideas found in one people's dreams may be very different from that found in another's. Moreover, literal, rather than symbolical, dreams also occur.

Naturally the character of the dreams very largely reflects the influence of higher cultural ideas that have been brought to bear on the conscious mind, though by no means to the exclusion of concepts more deeply embedded in the unconscious. The width of the gulf in cultural background is immediately evident if one compares the general tenor of the dreams of a people such as the Thai with those of the primitive agricultural peoples of Southeast Asia who have virtually escaped Chinese and Indian influences. A case in point would be the Nagas of Assam where, for some of the tribes, many of their typical dreams have been recorded. In the list given by T.C.Hodson one notes that the Thai and the Nagas only have in common a few physical dream occurrences, such as that to climb a hill or take a bath is fortunate, and the rather less obvious one that the loss of a tooth presages a death in the family.[1]

In the Bangkok National Library many dream books are preserved in the manuscripts department, and one comes across references to their use in classical Thai literature. However for the more complicated cases one finds the dreamer asking some more experienced elder for his interpretation, or in the case of royal dreams an astrologer. At the present day there appears to be no slackening in the demand, which I believe also exists in western countries, and printed compilations are always on sale in Bangkok. I now give a short selection,[2] which I have classified, but only roughly because of obvious overlapping.

Dream	Interpretation
Personal:	
Chanting *mantras* or hearing chanting.	Misfortunes averted.
Seeing an abbot preaching.	Will be very happy and well.
See a parent—alive or dead.	Trouble ahead; make merit to avert.
See a monk.	Happy and well; but not rich.
One is struck by lightning.	Disturbed because of a lord.
Feasting and drinking arrack.	Will not be well.
See oxen or buffaloes.	Tired in body and mind.
See clean or sweet rice.	Will be lucky.
Someone gives one a handkerchief.	Embarrassment; tears will flow.
Fall from house or tree.	Faced with ruin; must avert omen.
Eating honey.	Will be great and successful.
Taking a bath.	Will be cool and happy.
Resting on a comfortable bed.	Happy and trouble free.
Drinking water.	Future happiness; no more sorrow.
A house burning down.	Dissatisfaction with home; but if house someone else's can be viewed with complacency.
See a soothsayer.	Will be faced with problems.
Marital etc. relations:	
Given ring or hand ornaments.	Will obtain agreeable spouse; if married, good children.
Wearing violet.	Meet pleasing spouse.
Snake entwines arms and legs.	Will soon marry.
Drive away a poisonous snake after it bites.	Will obtain a very affectionate spouse.
See a pretty woman holding a light coming towards you.	Will get an agreeable wife. If a woman, a husband of position.
Moonlight.	Trouble over spouse.
Your house falls down.	Spouse will leave or die.[3]
Picking flowers.	Will obtain a good spouse.
See a snake.	Will meet a beloved.
Wearing a collar.	Going to be married.
Heart being torn out.	Will lose spouse.

Friends and relatives:

Front teeth break.	A relative will die.
Back teeth (molars) break.	Parent or near relative will die.
Arm or leg cut off.	Will lose a friend.
Eyeball torn out.	Will lose a beloved child.
Quarrel with friends.	Precisely that.
See *devatā*.	Friends (?) will slander.
See a host of insects.	Trouble with family and servants.
Quarrel with relatives.	They think of you and are coming.
Elephants and horses enter house.	Long separated relatives to be expected.
See a dog.	Will have good friends and no trouble.
See a cat.	Will spend money on helping others.
Quarrel with neighbours.	Exactly that.
Cutting flowers.	Will have good children.
Give birth to or otherwise obtain a child.	Good fortune.
Eating fruit.	News of distant friend or relative.

Occupational prospects:

Put in jail, or charged with crime.	Will change work, or be promoted.
Hands or feet cut with fetters.	Change of work, or employment.[4]
Blowing a trumpet or oboe.	Will have power and distinction.
Entering a new house.	Will obtain new work.
Sitting under a big tree.	Will become a person of authority.
Becoming a monk.	Good and respected, but poor.
Travelling.	Troubled with regard to future work.[5]
See shoes or put them on.	Must travel afar.
See a lotus flower.	Will have rank and bring honour to family.
Climbing a height, or white ant's hill.	Promotion coming.
See a temple or a palace.	Will become high official of great authority.
Falling from a high place.	Will lose honour and authority. A bad omen.
Travel by boat or carriage, running into storm.	Danger, don't go.
Sitting in boat or carriage.	Promotion coming.
See the king or queen.	Fortunate, promotion ahead.

DREAMS

Wealth and desire fulfilment:

Nāga entwines hands and feet.	Will receive help.
Picking fruit.	Will obtain desires.
Eating with parents and family.	Fortunate in every way.
Get or see a tortoise.	Will obtain a servant.
See drinking cups.	Will get an assistant.
Taking the air.	Will get something desired.
Little children come to sleep in the house.	Will get many slaves and become a noble.
Walking beneath a parasol.	Will gain by winning a wager.
See a teacher.	Will obtain your desire.
Collect uncountable sums of money.	Will obtain your desires.
Riding elephant, horse, ox or buffalo	Wealth, peace and happiness.
Someone brings gift of money.	Will receive money, but beware of swindler.
See green trees.	Will have plenty: rice, goods, money.
Put on new shoes.	Will get good, reliable servants.
See the moon.	Fortune from a noble.
See white elephant or white buffalo.	Will gain wanted possessions.

Loss of possessions:

Transplanting young padi.	Lose valued possessions; trouble.
See bird of prey.	As above.
See withered leafless tree.	As above.
Cutting hair or nails.	Will lose money.
See dog carry off pot.	Will suffer a theft.

Enemies slander or plan evil:

Wearing red.	Enemies will plot against you.
Sit in boat, crossing water.	Enemies plot but cannot get at you.
Chased by tiger, elephant or bear.	Will encounter an enemy planning evil.
Get a hat, or don one.	A great man will protect from enemies.
Beaten by someone.	Will be slandered.

Enemies defeated:

Wearing new clothes.	Will happily triumph over enemies.

See a Buddha image.	Will have power over enemies.[6]
See the sun.	Power and authority, enabling you to defeat any enemies.

Lawsuits or court charges:

See spirit or demon.	Will be accused in court.
Someone ties you up.	As above.
See nobles.	Will be tried in cour and found guilty.[7]
See a charcoal fire.	As above.

Horror or extreme anxiety (omens reversed):[8]

Contemplate rotting, offensive material.	Will gain wealth.
Being murdered.	Will gain wealth and defeat enemies.
You are dead and being carried away.	Will live long; if ill, will recover.
Stabbed and disembowelled.	Will be great; feared by enemies.
See dying person or corpse.	Finish with the bad and change for the better.
See own body putrefying.	Will receive news from opposite sex.
Weeping.	Will finish with all troubles.

A few dreams famous in Thai literature and history exhibit a greater degree of originality than the above, though not necessarily of veracity. However the simple dream of the serpent entwining itself about a bride or bridegroom-to-be occurs twice in Sunthon Phu's celebrated classic, the *Story of Phra Abhai Mani*. The first occasion was when the young heroine Kaew Kesra discovered from the dream book which she kept by her bedside that it indicated a love-match. As this was not precisely what she was desiring at the time, she flung the book down in anger. Later we are told of a king Laman who was mourning the loss of a beloved queen when he dreamt that a fire-breathing serpent descended from on high, coiled itself round his palace and burnt both it and the king to ashes. Sending for his astrologers his suspicions were confirmed that it meant that he would soon have a new consort.[9]

The most famous example of a premonitory dream of a coming birth is to be found in the great historical novel *Khun Chang Khun*

Phan. In the case of the birth of Khun Chang, the mother dreamt that a large bald-headed vulture flew into her room carrying in its beak the decaying corpse of a huge elephant and that these two entered her side. The baldness of the vulture, the lady's husband was able to explain, signified that the child would be bald throughout life, while the elephant indicated riches. On the other hand the mothers of the other chief personages in the poem received more agreeable portents in that in each case a *deva* brought the mother-to-be a beautiful ring, which again the respective husbands were well able to interpret. One of the better favoured children was to be the future Khun Phan, the other a girl named Pim, later Wan Tong. Eventually they married and, in circumstances not necessary here to relate, Wan Tong had an alarming nightmare. In this she dreamt that the mosquito net caught fire, her bedfellow was consumed and she jumped from the burning bed badly seared. The interest is that Khun Phan's interpretation gives an excellent example of reversing the omen, as was usual in such cases. The fire that burnt the curtain announced good, not evil, and meant that wickedness had been destroyed. An enemy was defeated!

I conclude with mention of the celebrated dream of King Naresuen, as recorded in the *Annals*, on the night prior to his victory over the Burmese Crown Prince in 1592.

At 4 a.m. the king dreamed that he was moving in a boat over a great flood that had come through the western forest and that he was there attacked by a huge crocodile, which he killed. On awakening he informed the astrologer. The latter explained that there would indeed be a great battle, and the king would fight a fierce elephant duel, but would win and would destroy his enemy. The king was very pleased at this prediction.[10]

NOTES TO CHAPTER IX

1 T. C. Hodson, *The Naga Tribes of Manipur*, London, 1911, p. 130f.
2 From *BSMB* pp. 239–244.
3 According to the Satow MS. favourable dreams when house building are of people singing, carrying a child (on the hip) to draw water, leading in oxen or buffaloes to be yoked.
4 Formerly most Thai men preferred to leave the more arduous toil to immigrant Chinese.
5 Apart from the dangers associated with travel, for the official class it often meant separation from relatives and the comforts of the capital for a less healthy provincial environment.
6 Individual Buddha images often become celebrated for their supposed magical power.
7 In earlier times the sight of a noble or high official could, not unnaturally, be associated with the idea of oppression.
8 In keeping with the Thai temperament, though it is also found elsewhere, in the worst nightmares the omens are interpreted as the reverse of what would be expected.
9 *The Story of Phra Abhai Mani*, trans. by H.H.Prince Prem Purachatra, Bangkok, 1959, pp. 36, 102.
10 *Annals of Ayudhyā*, in Thai, Bangkok, 1913, Vol. I, p. 151.

CHAPTER X

DAYS OF DESTINY

For the Thai, as for most people, New Year is the occasion for serious concern as to what Fate may have in store for the next twelve months. However the Thai have three New Years, the modern solar introduced in 1889 and falling always on 1st April, the old lunar beginning on the first day of the waxing of the fifth month, when the animal name of the duodenary cycle is changed, and the Hindu-imported old solar astrological reckoning. According to the last-mentioned the New Year starts on the date of the sun's supposed entry into Aries, 13th April, the first day, known as Mahā-sankrānti, of a three days' festival. From the point of view of divination, it is only this festival that must be taken into consideration, the Days of Destiny *par excellence*.

This is not because the majority of people have any knowledge of astrology beyond the general recognition that the passage of the sun into Aries is fraught with danger for the world at large. It is partly because the Brahmans have so arranged matters as to associate the announcement of their prognostications for the coming harvest with this great day. Then there is much more of ultimately Indian origin in the popular tradition that at dawn a Songkrant angel arises in the eastern sky and by her appearance signifies what the future holds. The inscriptions forming the well-known encyclopaedia in stone of Wat Po, Bangkok, ascribe the tradition to Pāli sources coming from the Môns of Burma.[1] They tell of the Brahman sage Kapila and how he lost his head in a wager. The head had to be borne aloft, and each year as the sun enters Aries one of his seven daughters as the Songkrant angel flies round Mount Meru bearing her father's head. An explanatory myth, no doubt, but what really matters to the people is the particular angel it is, and the portents associated with her. All of which really depends, or so says our treatise, on which day of the week is 13th April.

Sunday. The angel is named Dungṣa, she wears pomegranate flowers behind the ears, is adorned with precious stones and is eating figs. In her right hand she has a discus, in her left a conch, and she rides a Garuda. That year cultivated rice will not do very well.

Monday. The angel is Gorāga, and she wears behind the ears the flowers of *Mayodendron* sp. *(Bignonaceae)*, is adorned with pearls and eats butter. In her right hand she has a sword, in the left a staff, and she rides a tiger. That year there will be trouble for ministers and nobles.

Tuesday. The angel, named Rākṣasa, wears royal lotus, is adorned with precious stones and is drinking blood. In her right hand she holds a trident, in her left a bow, and she rides a boar. That year there will be danger to the country, fire, robbery and much illness.

Wednesday. The angel named Maṇḍā wears *Champa* flowers, is adorned with brilliant gems, and is eating butter. In her right hand she holds a needle, in her left a staff, and she rides an ass. The king will receive presents from foreign countries, but weak children will die.

Thursday. The angel named Kiriṇī wears *maṅḍā* flowers, is adorned with emeralds, and is eating sesame. In her right hand she has a sickle, in her left a gun, and she rides an elephant. A high church dignitary will die, and the abbots will be disturbed.

Friday. The angel named Kimidā wears small white *Nymphaea* blooms, is adorned with topaz, and is eating bananas. In her right hand she has a sword, in her left a guitar, and she rides a buffalo. Rice and fruits will be abundant; but there will be frequent tempests, children will be lost, and there will be much eye trouble.

Saturday. The angel is Mahodhara, she wears water hyacinths, is adorned with sapphires and eats deer flesh. In her right hand she has a discus, in her left a trident, and she rides a peacock. Portents as for Tuesday.[2]

In view of such gloomy forebodings one might suppose that a general feeling of despondency might now be abroad, but in fact that is far from being the case, since everyone knows that there are two more days of predictions to come. However on *wan nao*, the second day of the festival, little in the way of comfort is offered. If *wan nao* is a

Sunday: The padi crop will die and one will hear the voices of foreigners, while the nobles are upset.
Monday: Salt will be dear, there will be much illness, and the nobles disturbed.
Tuesday: Areca, betel rice and fish will be dear, and the officials despondent.
Wednesday: Rice and fish will be dear; everyone disturbed, and the widows leaving home.
Thursday: Fruit will be dear, and the royal family will be much disturbed.
Friday: Pepper will be dear. Birds of prey will die suddenly, and jungle animals will suffer calamities. Widows will inherit property.
Saturday: Padi will wither owing to scarcity of water. Rice, vegetables and fish will all be dear. There will be fire in the city. Nobles will do wrong, and Brahmans will suffer.[3]

Surprisingly enough no one is unduly disturbed. The Tha people, as we have seen, live in the expectancy that evil omens can be averted or at least superseded by later predictions, and on this third day of the New Year festival they are not disappointed. For this is the New Year's Day proper, the day on which the serial number of the year is changed, known as *wan talöng sok*. With an essentially light-hearted people it is now just a question of joyfully contemplating which particular beneficent outlook the day will indicate, though for the state and rulers rather than for the people.

Sunday: The king will be great and prosperous. He will conquer his enemies in all directions.
Monday: The queen and royal ladies will enjoy every happiness.
Tuesday: The officials will be completely happy; even if there is war in some direction the Thai will be victorious.
Wednesday: The royal *pandits*, *purohita* and astrologer will enjoy calm and every sort of happiness.
Thursday: The Brahmans will tranquilly attend to their religious duties.

Friday: Those who trade with foreign countries will be well pleased with their profits.

Saturday: The courageous Thai soldiers will be contented; should they have to fight they will be victorious.[4]

The above prognostications, both good and bad, bear the stamp of the pre-modern period when pepper was a valuable export and the status of the Brahmans still exalted. It was on the first day of the festival that, as mentioned on page 89, the Brahmans made their predictions as to the rainfall for the coming season. They also announced which would be the lucky and unlucky days of the week throughout the year.[5] But as these were obtained by simple numerical calculations fully explained in the treatises it is not surprising that nowadays most people could acquire such information independently, or just by consulting the printed calendars.

Most important, in the negative sense, are the Days of Universal Destruction *(Lokavināsana)*. Take as an example the Chula year 1342 (A.D. April 1979–April 1980). To find the day you add 1120 = 2462, then divide by 7 which gives 351, remainder 5, so that Thursdays during the year will be *lokavināsana*. If you wish to know the watch, you divide by 8, if you wish to know the $rksa$, or asterism of the lunar day, you divide by 27, in each case taking the remainder.

Positively, it is just as important to know the days of the Victorious Flag, or *Wan Dho'n Jaya*, when Rāhu and Mṛtayu (Death) are not wandering about. As for example in the same year Chula 1342. Multiply by 10 = 13420. Add 1 = 13421 and then divide by 7 = 1917, remainder 2, so that the *Wan Dho'n Jaya* is Monday. To find the watch or the $rksa$ divide the figure 13421 by 8 or 27, in each case taking the remainder. For the Upāsana, another ill-omened day or $rksa$, multiply the Chula year by 10 and add 2, then make similar divisions to find the remainders.[6]

Then the treatise explains a method for finding out whether any particular day *(rksa)* of the lunar month is auspicious. For this method one must bear in mind that the week-days are not numbered in the usual order, but as follows: Sunday 6, Monday 2, Tuesday 5, Wednesday 1. Thursday 4, Friday 7, Saturday 3. One then takes the number of the present month—if there is an intercalary month in the year one counts from the fifth month as one, if there is not, one counts from the sixth month as one. Multiply the number of the present month, as thus counted, by 2 and add the number of days of the month up to the present day. If this comes to more than 27, subtract 27. Add the number of the day of the week according to the above given enumeration, and then divide by 7. The remainder gives the omen: 1, 2 or 3 inauspicious; 4, 5 or 6 auspicious. We may take as an example the 20th day, a Thursday, of the 12th month, which counts as month 8 starting from the fifth month in a year which has an intercalary month. So 8 multiplied by $2 = 16+20$ (days) $= 36-27$, leaves 9. Add 4 (Thursday) $= 13$ which being divided by 7 gives a remainder of 6, which is an auspicious number.[7]

Another way to determine whether any given day would be auspicious for any important undertaking is to measure a stick by the middle finger of your right hand. Its length should be in accordance with the day. If it is a Sunday, measure on the stick 3 joints, if Monday 12 joints, if Tuesday 14 joints, if Wednesday 17 joints, if Thursday 12 joints, if Friday 11 joints, if Saturday 10 joints. Then use the measured stick for drawing a circle on the ground and set it up in the middle of the circle. If the shadow of the stick falls within the circle the day is auspicious.[8]

As there are many different kinds and degrees of both lucky and unlucky days it is necessary when planning important (auspicious) occasions to be much more specific than is allowed by either of the above approximations. The necessary instructions are provided in the treatise known as *Tamrā wong*, treatise of loops.[9] This has diagrams, one for each day of the week, each made up of a number of curiously arranged loops or belts, some of which cut one another at different angles (page 129). Traversing these vertically are three parallel rows of figures which start at the top right, from whichever is the number of the day, and continue down to the bottom of the diagram. When the number seven is reached they start again, and after reaching the bottom of the column they begin again from the top of the next column, so that all the days of the month are marked on the diagram. To find out whether the day you have in mind is lucky or otherwise for planning an auspicious occasion, be it house-building, a wedding or a top-knot cutting, you choose the diagram for the day which coincides with the first of the waxing of the month you are considering. You count from that day until you reach the lunar day you have in mind. Against many of the days is inscribed a word signifying its lucky or unlucky character, from which of course one is well advised to choose only those of the former indication. Here I have thought it sufficient to show only two of the day diagrams, which will enable one to see how the days of good or ill omen are distributed. I now give a list of these daily omens, together with the definition of each as given in the treatise. As Gerini gave some attention to these portents in his work on the Tonsure Ceremony I have thought it of interest to add in brackets his interpretation of each presage.[10]

Amr̥gajog or *Mahāsiddhijog (joga)*: prosperity, victory (*Amrityayoga*, free from deadly influences, highly successful moment).

Itthi patta: fire will burn house (*Itthi panāsa*, placed under a constellation of feminine name—harmful).

Ayopannasa: will have many enemies, must be armed (*Ayota panāsa*, danger from enemies and wild beasts.)

Kaladan: will have many punishments, and ruin from nobles (*Kaladanda* of Death's punishment; penalties from rulers, or fatal falls from trees).

Daradik: will have difficulties and poverty throughout life. (*Daradika* terrible, dreadful; if one travels by water will be wrecked and drowned.)

Mr̥tayū: much serious disease (*Mrittyu*, infested with plague and other calamities).

Dinasūña (*Dinasunya*, the day of the sun's transition between two signs.)

Dakadin: will lose wealth (*Dakshadina*, of bad disposition).

Yamakhan: sorrow from punishment by friends. (*Yamakhanda*, infested with plague etc.).

On such *apamaṅgala* days one cannot find happiness, and on *wan pòt* (blind days) the quest for it is equally in vain. Gerini also gives as lucky days *jaya yoga*, victorious moment; and *mahā jaya yoga*, highly victorious or propitious time, He recognizes that the Thai word *chok (jog)*, Páli and Sanskrit *yoga*, originally meant a conjunction of planets, particularly that of the Moon with each

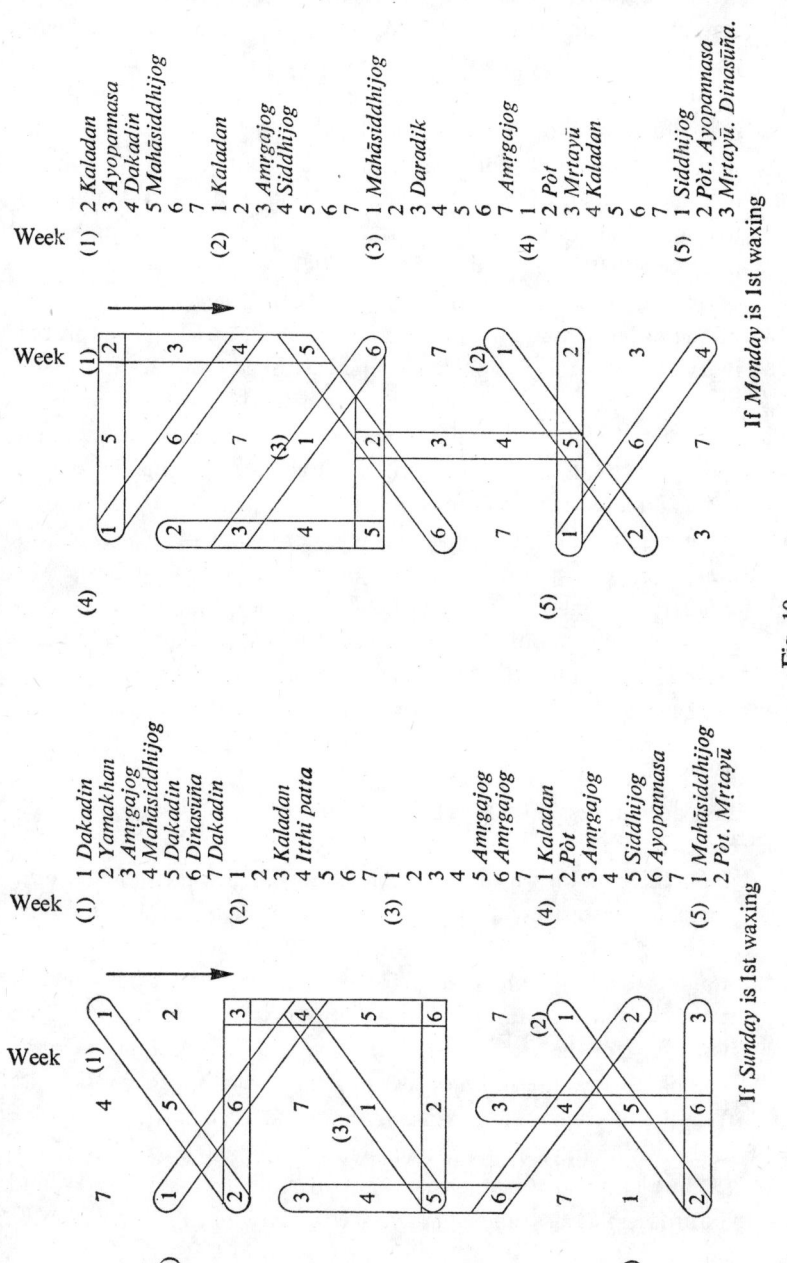

Fig. 10

of the 27 lunar asterisms or *nakṣatras*. Here it has come to mean simply a conjunction of the lunar days with the week days. These propitious days, though not all specifically mentioned in the text of our treatise, are all marked on the loop diagrams with which it is illustrated. It should be added that, according to our text, while it is fortunate for a number to be contained in one loop, it is unlucky to be caught in more than one, proportionately up to a maximum of four, which is fatal. In addition to these diagrams in former days a table showing the lucky and unlucky days was often engraved on a small ivory plate, called *dakadin*. A number of such plates, some with decorated borders, are displayed in the ivory room in the Bangkok National Museum.

A good example from literature of attention to these precepts is provided in the story of *Khun Chang Khun Phan*, when Khun Phan chose an auspicious time for making his magic sword. It was on a Saturday that coincided with a *mahāsiddhijog*.[11] On the other hand we find in the much older work the *Chronicle of Lamphun*, a suggestion that the original astrological basis was more fully comprehended. On a certain occasion an order was given to some monks to invoke the *devas* 'on a propitious day marked by a constellation of good omen, *amittajoka*.'[12]

The curious circumstance may be mentioned here that for the state ceremony of the First Ploughing it is laid down that all such lucky and unlucky days as are given above are to be ignored. Instead a series of days and dates are given from which an auspicious date for the ceremony must be selected, this series being apparently unknown in other connections.[13] I suggest that it may have been introduced from India in association with this ceremony.

The calendar is further complicated by one week-day each month, starting from Sunday for the fifth month, being denominated as floating (auspicious); while one week-day, starting from Thursday for the fifth month, is regarded as sinking (inauspicious). The other days are more or less neutral.[14] Again, certain days are friendly to each other, namely Sunday and Thursday, Monday and Wednesday, Friday and Tuesday, Wednesday afternoon (Rāhu) and Saturday. Other days are the reverse: Friday and Saturday, Tuesday and Sunday, Wednesday and Friday.[15]

NOTES TO CHAPTER X

1 H.H. Prince Dhani, 'The Inscriptions of Wat Phra Jetubon', *Journ of Siam. Soc.*, Vol. 26, p. 166. The Burmese and Cambodian versions differ in detail (Sangermano, op. cit., p. 210; Leclère, op. cit., p. 80). *BSMB*. pp. 219–222 reproduces the Thai text of the Kapila myth.
2 *B* I, p. 111.
3 ibid., p. 112.
4 ibid., p. 113.
5 This accords with the Brahmans' practice in India (see Dubois, op.cit., p. 137).
6 *B* I, pp. 116 f.
7 ibid., p. 91.
8 ibid., p. 90.
9 *B* II, pp. 89–96.
10 G.E. Gerini, *Chulakantamaṅgala*, Bangkok, 1893, p. 37.
11 *Khun Chang Khun Phan*, in Thai, Bangkok, 1917, Vol. II, pp. 44-46.
12 A. Notton, *Chronique de La: p'un*, Paris, 1930, p. 23.
13 H. G. Quaritch Wales, *Siamese State Ceremonies*, p. 256.
14 *B* I, p. 89.
15 *B* I, p. 42.

CHAPTER XI

WARS AND RUMOURS OF WARS

The Thai were to enjoy a long period of virtually unbroken peace after the British occupation of Rangoon in 1824 had finally removed the menace of Burmese aggression. They had been a sufficiently warlike people when in 1350 they threw off the yoke of the declining Khmer empire, and less than a hundred years later captured its capital, Angkor. But the Thai were to need all their warlike qualities to preserve their independence, first against their cousins the Lao states to the north, and then over a period of more than two centuries of continuous friction with the Burmese. This culminated in the great Burmese invasion which brought about the final destruction of Ayudhyā in 1767. A few years later a national saviour emerged in the person of King Tak. He drove out the Burmese and re-established the independence of Siam, just as the even more famous hero King Naresuen had done in similar circumstances in 1584.

Actually it was an unusually bold Thai incursion into Burma in 1662, during a period of internal unrest in that kingdom, that ushered in a relatively quiet interlude in the relations of the two countries. This led, as so often happens, to the Thai letting down their guard against their ultimately implacable enemy. With recovery and the establishment of the new capital at Bangkok, it soon came to be felt that it was not owing to any lack of military prowess that Ayudhyā had succumbed, but was rather due to the lack of proper attention accorded to such matters as ritual and prognostication. Two manuscripts, one of them dating from A.D. 1793, of the Thai *Treatise on the Art of War*, are preserved in the Bangkok National Library.[1] At the beginning of his reign the traditionally-minded King Rama III, in 1825 ordered the preparation of a new edition, in which any errors should be corrected. No copies of the new edition are known to have survived, but it is thought that Adolf Bastian, who gives a good deal of information differing from what is found in the 1793 *Treatise*, must have had access to the revised version. However it must be borne in mind that while the earlier version was probably written by Brahmans with personal knowledge of the Ayudhyan traditions, the later pandits were trying to correct something no longer perfectly understood; the additional information available from Bastian should therefore be regarded as a commentary, reflecting however the beliefs of the early nineteenth century.

The subject matter of the *Treatise* has been dealt with by me in detail against the whole background of war in Southeast Asia, but in a book which has long been out of print and is not generally accessible.[2] It may therefore be convenient to repeat here succinctly most of what I said on the subject of war prognostications. But, in view of our acquaintance with the generally more advanced methods of the Thai, it goes almost without saying that it was probably only such marginal peoples as the Laos who still had recourse to the drawing of augury from the examination of chicken bones.

First of all, wind direction should be taken into consideration, a wind blowing in the direction of the enemy being most favourable. A wind blowing from the left is favourable, but weapons must be held in the left hand. If it blows from both sides at once the army must stand firm with weapons held in *both* hands, and the men must also be able to manage the elephants and horses with both hands.[3] Of great importance are the following omens:

If you see a cloud break into many, with Meru form, don't march for it signifies death. The elephants and horses will vomit blood. The following visions and signs indicate that you will be beaten by the enemy: If it thunders and the wind blows in your face, don't move off, the elephants and horses will jump with fear. Also all the men will tumultuously dispute together. If you see a white garment turn coloured, green, violet and dark red, remember this sight isn't good, so don't go hastily. If objects lose their shadow, vessels of arrack break fortuitously, weapons fall from the hand of their own accord, then death lurks in the forest, so don't follow your intention. If a tree falls at your feet, don't consider this as nothing and don't dare to start. If a bird of prey comes flying softly, this points against marching, so don't go. For fighting you must await a favourable sign. Thus, if the wind blows from behind, you can beat the enemy quickly. If you see two crocodile forms together you will gain abundant wealth, obtain victory, and take the enemy's city. If you hear thunder continually behind you, attend to it, for it is the best sign. If you see clouds gather in the open space behind you it is an omen of glorious outcome; the enemy will be entirely defeated and you will prosper. A splendid and brilliant portent: if you hear the strains of music (conch, gongs etc.) start in answer to it, for it is propitious. Let all Brahmans, elephants and horses move off in order; it is a good time to start, so march at once and you will prosper and gain joy. If a bee flies noisily to and fro, quickly move off the army, go with strong forces and you will defeat the enemy.[4]

Now I will summarize the omens to be drawn from cloud movements, as apart from their shapes.[5] Significantly enough it is the clouds moving from north and west (Lao states and Burma) that are identified with the enemy, those from the south and east with the Siamese forces:

Favourable Cloud Movements

Clouds from N. moving S. not reaching sun
Clouds from W. moving E. not reaching sun
Clouds from S. moving W. overclouding sun
Clouds from E. moving W. overclouding sun

Unfavourable Cloud Movements

Clouds from N. moving S. overclouding sun
Clouds from W. moving E. overclouding sun
Clouds from S. moving N. not reaching sun
Clouds from E. moving W. not reaching sun

Just before he entered on his most decisive action, the *Annals* record that King Naresuen 'noticed a huge cloud coming up from the north-west. Then it returned and dispersed before it reached the sun, which remained clear and brilliant in the sky.'[6] And apart from thus watching the cloud movements a Thai commander had to be very careful, as in other important undertakings such as house-building (p. 72 above), to avoid facing the Nāga.[7]

The following is from the additional information recorded by Bastian, presumably from the 1825 edition of the *Treatise:*

If you see blood don't leave camp, or if a sword girdle snaps or a bow breaks, also not if insects float in the air or bees fly past and settle on swords and other weapons; their settling on musical instruments is a similar warning. Further, if horses and elephants get into confusion in the first or second night watches, don't start against the enemy, disaster if you do. Further, when you ought to be starting on the march and you see people dressed in white clothing looking as if they were dressed in black, then that is a sure foreboding of great loss of men; do not go further forward. When weapons fall out of the hands or other objects slip (or fall), then misfortune and defeat stand ahead; do not go further. If on the march you see clouds in the form of a Garuḍa this would mean defeat if you looked back. If you see a double pattern (in the clouds) then the king's council or the queen will die. If you see a triple one then you will win after a hard battle; a quadruple pattern means you will conquer. A quintuple pattern portends great losses among the nobles. If you see a sextuple one go no further or you'll be food for crows and vultures. If the men marching hear the call of a bird on their left, which then flies off and settles on a tree on the right-hand side, then great booty will be gained. But it is very unlucky if it settles on a tree stump or decayed trunk. If the bird comes flying past from the south-east and shrieks loudly while it is poised over the way, then misfortune is in its voice, for it says 'the enemy will be over you even before the day is ended.' If the bird flies on in front of and beyond our marching forces, then it is leading us forward.[8] Everyone must follow its lead with haste and spirit, for the enemy is certainly in that direction. According to the hour of day, animals coming from the right or left are propitious or the reverse.[9]

In addition, Bastian indicates that almost any pleasant or unpleasant sight seen immediately before a battle is taken to presage a favourable or unfavourable outcome.

If I were asked how much of this sort of thing could possibly survive in the era of modern warfare I should begin my reply by putting the question of divination in its wider context of Thai attitude to war in general. I should remember that in the old days a personal amulet was needed by every Siamese soldier high or low, also by elephants and horses. And I should then aver, without fear of contradiction, that today every Thai soldier in his desire for protection against enemy weapons is as careful to provide himself with a trusted amulet as his predecessor was of yore; and also, where it applies, one for his tank or armoured car, just as is the coach or lorry driver who ventures daily on Thailand's dangerous highways. But could a modern Thai officer, trained on the Western model, bring himself to glance at the cloud patterns as he went into battle? Yes, I think that he could, for Western influences and modernization do not penetrate to the roots in such matters. I well remember First World War British soldiers speaking with the utmost conviction about that remarkable apparition known as the Angel of Mons.

Many of the portents mentioned above belong to a class that are mentioned in the Thai manuscripts as occurring whenever the *devatā* wish to issue a warning. They are to be distinguished from sometimes similar supernatural manifestations which occur *concurrently* with noteworthy historical events. As such they are frequently mentioned in the *Annals*, but are to be considered as contemporary prodigies, not connected with divination.

The portents of possible war or more local calamity are held to show the displeasure of this or that Hindu deity, and the consequences can be averted by appropriate offerings. Typical examples of such portents are as follows: Lightning strikes houses, or rainbow pierces. Rice-pots fall from the hand, relatives quarrel without cause, domestic cattle run away, animals exhibit unnatural sexual behaviour, nobles fall to their deaths from elephants and palanquins. Protective house spirits forsake houses, and bees and wasps infest them. Fires start in houses, bananas flower unnaturally, people cannot sleep for the mice biting, dogs climb on roofs and laugh cheerfully like men, green frogs and toads come up into the house, as do owls and jungle fowl, snakes and wild oxen. Dogs have two-headed or two-bodied pups. Evil spirits annoy, laugh and cry. Plough oxen will not work, blood flows from white ant hills, swords and spears flower, musical instruments sound of themselves, and weapons, clash. Buddha images fall and blood or tears flow from their eyes. Wild animals are tame, horses and elephants are frightened, and vultures settle on houses. Clothes and pillows appear dark red, sun and moon appear on fire, rain falls but the air is not cooled, and there are clouds but no rain. Water dries up in the jars, trees break off though there is no tempest, dark clouds seen at night resemble elephants, horses, cattle, buffaloes, rhinos and lions. One hears sounds of indistinct voices, sugar flows of itself from canes, stones break in the hand, money disappears without being stolen. Fire burns clothes, water pots call out, little padi produces much rice and vice versa.[10]

This type of portent is very ancient and, so far as Siam is concerned, though considerably naturalized, is clearly of Indian origin. Close parallels are to be found in Varāhamihira (Chapter XLVI) where he confirms (3) 'The deities, displeased with men's sinful conduct, produce these portents, to paralyze which the ruler should order an expiation in his kingdom.' And while, as we know, this observer was far more concerned with heavenly phenomena than with those merely terrestrial, he admits (99) that 'A clever observer of portents, should he be even devoid of astronomical knowledge, will become a renowned man and a favourite of the king.'

I now select from Varāhamihira a few examples which approach most nearly some of the Thai omens, and for all of which he prescribes the necessary expiation. Thus:

(8) The falling into pieces without any assignable cause, the moving, sweating, weeping, talking and the like of the emblems of Śiva, of idols and shrines, tend to the destruction of ruler and land. (9) The breaking or coming down of an axle, wheel, yoke... bring no good to land and king. (23) On seeing weapons blaze, move, utter sounds, jump out of the sheath, tremble... one may predict that dreadful war and tumult is quickly approaching. (25) When boughs of trees on a sudden snap asunder, you may predict a warlike expedition. (26) A tree produces discord in the realm by blossoming out of season. (40) A continual rain during a week, and that out of season, is followed by the death of the sovereign. (56) Unnatural sexual behaviour of animals. (61) When musical instruments sound without being struck... the foe is approaching or the king about to die. (63) Where ox and plough get entangled ... there is danger from the sword. (66, 67) Town birds roaming in the forest and wild birds entering the town without marks of fear; day birds roaming by night and nocturnal ones by day... all these bring danger. (68, 69) Threatening also are dogs wailing, as it were at the door; jackals yelling in vexed condition; a dove or owl penetrating into a palace; a cock crowing at eve. (74) The falling down or breaking of Indra's standard, of door-bolts, columns,

gates... foreshows the king's death. (79) That house meets ruin which is motley with cobwebs, not honoured at morn and evening, filled with quarrels... (80) When goblins show themselves you may predict pestilence.

All such manifestations, and the list of them could be greatly extended, simply indicate some disturbance of the natural order, consequent it would seem upon some misbehaviour by the people. Fortunately the Thai are generally so well ordered as to give no cause for divine complaint, and even more fortunately, were that to occur, the possibility of carrying out acts of expiation is always available. However it must be said that when in August 1975 the great main reliquary of That Phanom, the most revered Buddhist sanctuary in the north-east, the most politically sensitive part of the kingdom, collapsed, there was widespread consternation. The Fine Arts Department hastened to allay fears by ascribing the collapse to inadequate repairs at an earlier period, and proceeded to restore the monument.

For what Varāhamihira called 'celestial portents' we have a great deal of evidence but it may be considered somewhat indirect. That is because I take it mainly from the third part of the Cambodian manuscript of which we have already come to the conclusion that the two earlier parts were borrowed from the Thai.[11] It is indeed not possible to imagine that the Thai lacked such guidance, even though no Thai version has survived, so far as I am aware. The work is essentially Indian, as is shown from the mention of various place names, such as Madhurarāj (79D) and Pāñcāl (87B); but though ultimately rooted in such conceptions as those of Varāhamihira, it has evidently evolved a long way. One may also feel sure that it is the same treatise, or nearly the same, as that in use by the Burmese: according to Sangermano[12] the Burmese treatise has very similar deductions from the approaches of the planets to the Moon. To this extent, and in some other respects, this treatise may be considered rather more astrological than most of what we have previously met. It should be mentioned that this Cambodian manuscript does not concern itself with such frequent phenomena as eclipses, the occurrence of which Thai astrologers have always been able to predict. However in some other manuscripts one may find reference to prognostications to be drawn from the direction of Rāhu's supposed attack, extent of the eclipse and its duration.[13]

Of the celestial omens in the manuscript under consideration about one quarter of a total of some one hundred and sixty-eight appearances may be considered as auspicious, the great majority being decidedly the opposite. These usually presage dearth, civil disturbance or war, often a combination of all three. Of the favourable portents most concern rainfall, a few abundance and general well-being, while I have mentioned at the end of Chapter VII several that augur well for travel and trade. As regards the sun and moon the depictions in the manuscript are usually of a crudely geometrical form, the distinctions being made by each disc being made up of a core of one colour and a surrounding zone of another, often each with distinctive borders. The simple disc is often broken into by 'incursions' of one shape or another, thus extending the variety, while the Moon, often shown in crescent form, exhibits various deformities. The interpretations seem too arbitrary to make detailed examination worth while, so I shall content myself with a few examples below.

First, however, mention must be made of the various cloud forms which are usually more individually expressive, except where they are merely used as appendages to the Sun and Moon, often at the cardinal and sub-cardinal points. Reasonably enough it is the appearance of a cloud resembling lion, tiger or peacock that is the most suggestive of coming glory (69A), while one like the Sanskrit *śrī* syllable offers tranquillity (74C). On the other hand flames, a woman carrying a crocodile, a bull's head between masts, a drum or chowries, are indicative of war (70,71). Rainbows (74) are inauspicious, as generally with Varahamihira (Ch. XXXV).

Apart from deformities, often of the crescent, and variations in colour scheme, the Moon offers little in the way of individual design: shaped like a junk (82C) the yellow crescent presages alimentary abundance, wealth and peace; but a horse or camel on the red disc signify coming calamity (86A, B). For the Moon to resemble a yellow bird is favourable, less so if one sees it as two men carrying respectively a rabbit and a crocodile (86A, B). As already mentioned, the most eloquent evidence of the Indian influence is provided by the approaches of the planets (other than the Sun) to the Moon, as shown in 76A, 80A, 83C, D, E, in every case portending calamity, mostly war. According to Varāhamihira (IV, 21–26) the disastrous effect of a planet touching the Moon is felt only in the dark half of the month.

A few appearances of the Sun, of no particular interest in themselves, are considered favourable and pointing to rain; but they are the exceptions. Many of the representations, each disti nguhed by a different colour zoning, an associated cloud pattern or an 'incursion', mean such calamities as famine, banditry and war. Naturally the most interesting are those which show close connection with the indications of Varāhamihira: the Sun red above and green below, with a headless corpse coloured rose (49B); a red Sun disc with a blue crow on it (49 C); a red sun with a white umbrella (50A); a red Sun with a blue banner or a fan (50 B, C). These can all be closely paralleled in Varāhamihira (Chapter III). Perhaps most interesting of all is the statement (68 B, C) that if one sees *two* red or red-orange suns the king will be in danger or will be betrayed by bandits, while Varāhamihira (Ch. XLVII) has it that 'two suns forebode war between Ksatriyas; three, four or more suns, announce the world's end.'

Since the Thai have apparently lost their equivalent of the Cambodian manuscript, and consequently no printed editions have come into being to keep alive the memories of these dire predictions, it may be that all memory of them has disappeared from the urban Bangkok population. It might be a different matter with the villagers, especially those of the sensitive north-east, where traditions are better preserved in the folk memory, even if in course of time some misconceptions may have crept in. In support of this possibility I quote from a field observer in that area who gives us the following very pertinent information:

Said an old lady living not far from Roi Et in the North-east: 'I went to my land in a boat over the reservoir. This morning there were two suns in the sky, very bright, one on each side. It will be dry for a long time. This is an unlucky sign. Have you ever seen such a thing?'... The serious wondering voice of the old lady echoed in our minds. For her the two suns were fact, not metaphor or poetic description.[14]

During the first quarter of the present century the Thais had no cause for alarm. One may recall the words of Western-educated King Vajiravudh, soon after his accession in 1910, for his intensely modernizing reign of fifteen years. He has been called the father of Thai nationalism, but with his urge to spur the people forward he yet combined a respect for Thai traditions. I do not know to what extent he listened to the prognostications of the court astrologer, but I do know that he welcomed that auspicious appanage of royalty, a new white elephant, which made its appearance early in his reign. About the same time, when a provincial governor presented him some ancient Khmer bronze standards and other insignia that had recently been excavated, the king, and no doubt also the governor, saw them as something more than objects of archaeological interest. This is what his Majesty said:

During the first year of our reign several portents of the highest traditional import have made themselves manifest, and the augury they convey convinces us that prosperity, and not calamity, shall continue to be the lot of our Thai people. The discovery of the Monkey Standard, the Garuḍa Standard, and the bow and arrow of Rāma's strength, are sure manifestations that warriors have not yet ceased to exist in the land of the Thai, and inspire us all with confidence that the defence of our national independence will not be altogether futile. The appearance of the White Elephant at the same period is likewise a portent that the Kingdom of Siam will not fall to a low estate, unable to stand on an equal footing with the nations. All these portents have created a deep impression upon us, and we doubt not upon the minds of every one of you also.

At that time there was no reason to suppose that these encouraging predictions might perhaps bear a time limit.

NOTES TO CHAPTER XI

1. The text was printed and published by the Royal Institute, Bangkok, 1925.
2. H. G. Quaritch Wales, *Ancient South-east Asian Warfare*, London, 1952.
3. *Treatise on Ancient Warfare* (in Thai), p. 10.
4. ibid., pp. 10 ff.
5. ibid., pp. 8 ff.
6. *Annals of Ayudhya*, Vol. I, p. 157.
7. That the *nāga* concerned was the Śeṣa Nāga, or world serpent, was not understood by me when I wrote *Ancient South-east Asian Warfare*, p. 157.
8. An instance is given in the *Annals*, Vol. I., p. 35.
9. Bastian, op. cit., p. 481. On the next page he gives examples of calculations by the remainders methods of dates when victory of loss may be expected. Certain peculiarities suggest that these are derived from interpolations in the 1825 version of the war treatise.
10. *BSMB*, pp. 560–563. The descent of a vulture on a house roof is mentioned by Bastian (op. cit., p. 491) as an evil omen requiring the making of offerings; and it is equally recognized as 'a very threatening omen' in a present-day Thai village, according to B.J.Terwiel, op.cit., p. 178.
11. See above, Chapter II.
12. op. cit., p. 144.
13. Eclipse from the east, rice dear; from south-east, fires will break out; from south-west, banditry will prevail; from south, there will be dissatisfaction; from west, trouble for widows; from north-west, many animals will die; from north, happiness will prevail; from north-east, food plentiful (*B* III, p. 75). Portents from solar eclipse are similar (*BSMB*, p. 614).
14. Francis Cripps, *The Far Province*, London, 1965, p. 163.

GLOSSARY

Bāt — Thai monetary unit, or half-ounce weight.
Brahmā-devatā — an inhabitant of the higher Buddhist heavens.
Deva — a superior Hindu deity.
Devacara — the 'walking *devatā*', a minor deity who warns the traveller of danger.
Devatā — inferior Hindu deity or, in Buddhism, an angel.
Garuḍa — a type of semi-divine bird-man inhabiting a forest at the foot of Mount Meru, and constantly at war with the *nāgas*.
Hīnayāna — the 'Lesser Vehicle' or Southern Buddhism.
Jātaka — a Buddhist birth story, concerning a former life of the Buddha.
Ketu — in astronomy the descending node; considered as the ninth planet.
Khvăñ — Thai animistic spirit, resident in the individual's head; or, collectively, in the year tree.
Meru — the fabulous mountain at the centre of the world system, on the summit of which is the heaven of the inferior Hindu deities.
Nāgarāja — king of the *nāgas*.
Nāgas — semi-divine serpents, residents of the nether regions below Mount Meru.
Purohita — a royal chaplain.
Rāhu — in astronomy the ascending node, the cause of eclipses; considered as the eighth planet.
Rāmakien — Thai version of the Indian epic *Rāmāyaṇa*.
Śeṣa Nāga — the cosmic serpent, which supports the world system.
Stūpa — a Buddhist reliquary shrine.
Wat — a Thai Buddhist monastery.
Yakṣa — a demon or ogre, generally malevolent.
Yakṣī — a female demon or ogress.

INDEX

Agriculture, 87 ff.
Amulets, 135–6
Animal cycle, xi, 8, 19 ff., 63, 87
Animals, birth-, 8, 9 ff., 53 ff., 64 ff.
Animals, omens from, 78, 82 ff., 90, 93, 133, 136, 137, 141
Astrologers, astrology, ix, xi, 106, 123, 138, 141
Ayudhyā, xiii, 19, 132

Bangkok National Library, xii, xiii, xiv, 52, 116, 132
Bangkok National Museum, 130
Behaviour and posture, as portents, 111–2
Birds, as omens and portents, 78, 133, 135, 137
Boats, 92 ff.
Brāhmajāti, xii, xiii
British Library, xiv
British Museum, xiii
Burma, Burmese influence, xi, xiii, 52, 66, 73, 93, 132, 134, 138

Calendars, lunar and solar, xi, 123
Cardinal points, 33 ff., 75, 80
Celestial portents, 139
Childbirth, child-rearing, 3–5
China, Chinese influence, xi, 8, 52, 66, 116

Dakadin, 130
Days and dates, auspicious, x
  for agriculture, 91–2
  for boat-buying, 93
  for domestic life, 82
  for house-building, 72
  for tree-planting, 81–2
  for trading and travel, 93 ff.
  Victorious Flag, 126
Days of Universal Destruction, 126
Devabrahmā, 1

Devacara, 33, 34, 94, 97 ff.
Devas, descent of, 97 ff.
Dreams, 3, 116–21

Elements, birth-, 9, 63

Fate calculation, 8, 21 ff.
Fingers, finger-nails, 58–61
Five-tier system, see Numbers

Gardens, 80–2

Harvest, predictions for, 87–91
Horary method, 105 ff.
Horoscopes, ix, 36, 105 ff.
House-building, 72–80
Hpēwān, xi

India, Indian influence, ix, 8, 41, 48, 52, 73, 77, 101, 116, 130, 137

Jātakas, 8, 9, 13, 14, 15, 17

Ketu, x, 98
Khun Chang Khun Phan, 52, 120–1, 130
Knots (in timber), 77, 93

Lamphun, Chronicle of, 130
Law, lawsuits, 7
Lokabrahmā, 1–2
Lot-casting, see Sortilege

Mahā-sankrānti, 123
Manu, 1
Marriage, 63–70
Māyāmataya, 73

Nāga, Sēṣa, see Sēṣa Nāga
Name, choice of, 4

Naresuen, King, 121, 132, 134
New Year, 123 ff.
Numbers, numerical systems, 3, 19, 24 ff., 29, 31–2, 72, 89, 128

Offerings, 47
Ordeals, trial by, 112–4

Palmistry, 52–61
Parasol, three-staged, 36 ff.
Phra Abhai Mani, story of, 120
Phya Sattalung, 10
Pimples, 47–50
Planetary deities, x, 3, 4, 47, 89
Planets ruling age, 40–7
Ploughing, First Ploughing ceremony, 91, 130
Prasna Tantra, 105–6, 111
Precepts, eight, 1–2

Rāhu, x, 33, 36, 41 ff., 98 ff., 139
Rama III, King, 132
Rāmakien, Rāmāyana, 10, 40, 69, 95, 96, 114
Rāma's progress, 95–6
Recovery of lost property, 104 ff.
Remainder method, 3, 31, 67, 89

Satow, Sir Ernest, xiii
Séṣa Nāga, 77–8, 93, 134
Sickness, 111
Sleep, sleeping positions, 2–3

Soil, portents in, 75
Soothsayers, xi
Sortilege, x, 32
Sri Mahu Bodhi Divination Institution, xii–xiii

Tak, King, 114, 132
Tamra wong, see Treatise of Loops
That Phanom, 138
Theft and thieves, 104 ff.
Three-tier system, see Numbers
Trade, 92 ff.
Travel, 92 ff.
Treatise of Loops, 127–30
Treatise of Seven Numbers, 24 ff., 72 ff.
Treatise on the Art of War, 132
Trees, auspicious and inauspicious, 80–1
Twitches, 84

Vajiravudh, King, 141
Varāhamihira, 48, 50, 73, 80, 137–40

War, 132 ff.
Watch systems, 106 ff.
Wat Po, 123
Weather as portent, 88 ff., 102, 133–4, 139 ff.
Week (Indian origin), 9

Zodiac, signs of, x, 32–4, 36